AI and ML in Pharmaceutical Sciences

AI and ML in Pharmaceutical Sciences

Harish Dureja
M. Pharm., Ph.D. (Gold-Medalist)
Dean, Faculty of Pharmaceutical Sciences
Former Head, Department of Pharmaceutical Sciences
Director, Centre for IPR Studies
Director, Professional Consultancy Cell
Maharshi Dayanand University, Rohtak
Haryana, INDIA.

Visiting Professor
ARCCIM, Faculty of Health
University of Technology Sydney
NSW 2007 Australia.

Pharma Med PRESS An Imprint of BSP Books Pvt. Ltd.

(TM) **PharmaMed Press**
An imprint of BSP Books Pvt. Ltd.
4-4-309/316, Giriraj Lane,
Sultan Bazar, Hyderabad - 500 095.

AI and ML in Pharmaceutical Sciences
***by* Harish Dureja**

Published by:

PharmaMed Press

An imprint of BSP Books Pvt. Ltd.
4-4-309/316, Giriraj Lane, Sultan Bazar, Hyderabad - 500 095.
Phone: 040-23445688; Fax: 91+40-23445611
e-mail: info@pharmamedpress.com
www.pharmamedpress.com/pharmamedpress.net

ISBN: 978-93-48734-43-3 (Hardback)

Dedicated in the

Loving Memory of My Father

Preface

The field of pharmaceutical sciences is entering in to the exciting phase driven by rapid advancements in Artificial Intelligence (AI) and Machine Learning (ML). These advanced technologies are reshaping the different aspects of drug discovery & development, drug delivery and many more offering opportunities to make the process more precise, efficient and innovative. Within this evolving landscape, the book "AI and ML in Pharmaceutical Sciences" finds its purpose and significance.

This book is intended to address the growing need to understand the applications of AI and ML in pharmaceutical research and practice. This book serves as a comprehensive resource for a wide range of readers including researchers, industry professionals and students who are keen to learn about this exciting area of innovation.

The content of this book has been structured in a way that it is easy to follow with each chapter starting with an introduction to the main concepts and finally the mind map/graphical abstract. This approach helps the reader to familiarize themselves with the topic before diving deeper into more complex ideas.

The book is filled with various helpful tools to enhance the learning experiences. These include flowcharts, tables, mind map, point by point summary and key questions. The mind maps serve to simplify complex ideas and help the readers to quickly grasp key concept. The content is presented systematically using a clear structure with different headings and sub-headings. This makes an easy way for the readers to navigate through the material and find the information.

I wish to express my appreciation to the contributors who played crucial role in bringing up this book. I also welcome feedback from the readers as I believe that critical comments and suggestions are essential for improving the quality of this book. I hope that this book will serve as a valuable resource for students, educators and professional in the pharmaceutical sciences who are seeking interest in the exciting potentials of Artificial Intelligence and Machine Learning.

Harish Dureja
Rohtak

Contributors Affiliations

Prof. Anju Dhiman, Department of Pharmaceutical Sciences, Maharshi Dayanand University, Rohtak (Haryana), India.

Ms. Annu Saini, Department of Pharmaceutical Sciences, Maharshi Dayanand University, Rohtak (Haryana), India.

Mr. Gagan Dua, Department of Pharmaceutical Sciences, Maharshi Dayanand University, Rohtak (Haryana), India.

Ms. Honisha, Department of Computer Science and Engineering, Manipal University, Jaipur (Rajasthan), India.

Prof. Harish Dureja, Department of Pharmaceutical Sciences, Maharshi Dayanand University, Rohtak (Haryana), India.

Mr. Harshil Dureja, Electrical Engineering Department, Delhi Technological University, Delhi, India.

Mr. Lokesh Sharma, Department of Pharmaceutical Sciences, Maharshi Dayanand University, Rohtak (Haryana), India.

Mr. Lokesh Nagar, Department of Pharmaceutical Sciences, Maharshi Dayanand University, Rohtak (Haryana), India.

Ms. Nisha Gulati, Department of Pharmaceutical Sciences, Maharshi Dayanand University, Rohtak (Haryana), India.

Dr. Swagat Tripathy, TAP Pharmaceuticals AG (Maharashtra), India.

Mr. Tarif Hussian, Department of Pharmaceutical Sciences, Maharshi Dayanand University, Rohtak (Haryana), India.

Ms. Vaishali Saini, Department of Pharmaceutical Sciences, Maharshi Dayanand University, Rohtak (Haryana), India.

Mr. Vishal Vats, Department of Pharmaceutical Sciences, Maharshi Dayanand University, Rohtak (Haryana) India.

Contents

Preface ..... (vii)
Contributors Affiliations ..... (ix)

Chapter 1

Introduction of AI and ML in Pharmaceutical Sciences

Vishal Vats, Lokesh Sharma, Honisha, Vaishali Saini, Anju Dhiman, Tarif Hussian and Harish Dureja

1.1 Introduction 1
1.2 Artificial Intelligence (AI) 2
1.3 Machine Learning (ML) 8
1.4 Deep Learning (DL) 12
1.5 Neural Network (NN) 13
1.6 Data Types and Resources 14
1.7 Data Management 17
1.8 History of AI and ML in the Pharmaceutical and Healthcare Sector 19
1.9 Opportunities and Challenges of AI and ML in Pharmaceutical Sciences 22
1.10 Digital Technology Trends in the Pharmaceutical Industry 25
Proposed Questions 27

Chapter 2

AI and ML in Pharmaceutical Research and Development

Tarif Hussian, Gagan Dua, Lokesh Nagar, Anju Dhiman and Harish Dureja

2.1 Introduction 30
2.2 AI and ML Derived Drug Discovery 31
2.2.1 Drug Target Identification, Selection and Prioritisation with compound Screening and design 32
2.3 Random Forest (RF) and Naive Bayesian (NB) in Pharmaceutical Research and Development 36
2.3.1 Naive Bayesian (NB) 37
2.3.2 Support Vector Machines (SVMs) 37

2.4 Virtual Screening (VS) 38
2.5 Prediction of Safety, Efficacy and Toxicity (SET) 39
Proposed Questions 41

Chapter 3

AI and ML in the Modern Pharmaceutical Sector

Lokesh Nagar, Annu Saini, Tarif Hussian, Nisha Gulati and Harish Dureja

3.1 Introduction 44
3.2 Importance of AI and ML in Pharmaceuticals 46
3.3 Role of Pharmacist in the Modern Pharmaceutical Sector 47
3.4 AI/ML Based Medical Devices (MDs) 49
3.4.1 Digital Therapeutics (DTx) 53
3.5 AI/ML for Medical Imaging and Analysis 53
3.6 AI and ML for Predictive Maintenance and Remote Monitoring 55
3.7 AI/ML for Patient Monitoring and Signal Analysis 56
3.8 AI/ML Transformation in Pharmaceuticals with Robotics 57
3.9 AI/ML- Driven Wearable Technology and Biosensors 59
3.10 AI/ML in Pharmaceutical Supply Chain Management 63
Proposed Questions 66

Chapter 4

AI and ML in Clinical Care and Healthcare Operations

Nisha Gulati, Swagat Tripathy, Tarif Hussian, Lokesh Nagar and Harish Dureja

4.1 Introduction 70
4.2 AI and ML for Diagnostics and Prognosis 70
4.3 Electronic Health Records (EHR) with AI/ML Clinical Decision Support (CDS) 75
4.4 AI/ML for Disease Surveillance and Outbreak Decision 77
4.5 Resource Allocation and Capacity Planning with AI and ML in Healthcare Sector 78

4.6 AI and ML in Clinical Evaluation of Drugs, Devices and Software 79

4.7 AI & ML in Clinical Development: Real-World Patient Data Analysis 80

4.8 Decentralised Clinical Trials (DCTs) 81

Proposed Questions 82

Chapter 5

Future of AI and ML in Pharmaceutical Sciences and Healthcare

Honisha, Tarif Hussian, Harshil Dureja, Swagat Tripathy and Harish Dureja

5.1 Introduction 85

5.2 Pharmaceutical Industry 4.0 85

5.3 Digital Health Initiatives (DHIs) and Pharmaceutical Regulatory Environment 90

5.4 World Health Organization (WHO): Ethics and Governance of Artificial Intelligence for Health 93

5.5 Digital Health vs. e-Health 94

5.6 e-Prescription 96

5.7 Telemedicine 97

5.8 Digital Health Intervention (DHI) 99

5.8.1 Digital Health Interventions for Persons 99

5.8.2 Digital Health Interventions for Healthcare Providers (HCPs) 102

5.8.3 Digital Health Interventions for Health Management and Support Personnel (HMSP) 103

5.8.4 Digital Health Interventions for Data Services 105

5.9 Digital Health Interventions - Case Studies 106

5.9.1 U-report/UNICEF Uganda Strategy - Ebola Outbreak (August 2012) 106

5.9.2 Ayushman Bharat Digital Mission (ABDM) 106

5.9.3 Robotics Middleware for Healthcare (RoMi-H) in Singapore Public Health Institutions 107

5.9.4 Transforming Pneumonia Care: CAPE AI Predictive Engine ... 107

5.9.5 CoWIN - Revolutionizing Vaccination Through Digital Innovation in India ... 108

5.10 Digital Data Safety ... 108

5.11 Data Privacy Impact on the Pharmaceutical Sector ... 111

Proposed Questions ... 112

Further Readings ... **115**

List of Abbreviations ... **135**

CHAPTER 1

Introduction of AI and ML in Pharmaceutical Sciences

1.1 Introduction

The current era of digital technology is witnessing advancements in all the fields. The latest cutting-edge technologies have been integrated into our daily routine and provided the convenience and opportunities. The ease of communication in today's world through smartphone and the accessibility of knowledge using the internet are the simplest examples of digitalization. Data plays a vital role across all domains of this digital world. It is indispensable for modern economics and helpful in driving innovation and the decision-making process. The analogue information is turned into digital formats. The data (text, image, audio, video and many more) can be processed, transmitted and stored when represented using binary code (0s and 1s). By means of digitalization, the information can easily be analyzed and further shared via electronic devices and systems. The large amount of digital data can easily be handled using Artificial Intelligence (AI).

AI is a set of technologies that are used to make systems and programs perform the act or do the things that usually require human effort. The AI system simulates human learning and thinking ability, solving problems, understanding the language and ability to see things. The AI can find the patterns of the data, handle large amounts of data and make recommendations. The AI can be used for virtual helpers, understanding language, self-driving cars and personalized suggestions.

A subset of AI is Machine Learning (ML), where algorithms and models are developed using the data and make the decisions and predictions. The labeled or unlabelled data can be utilized by ML algorithms (without being programmed) to identify patterns, relationships and trends as well. The feedback and experience can improve the performance over time. Supervised learning (SL), unsupervised learning (UL), semi-supervised learning (SSL) and reinforcement learning (RL) are utilized by ML techniques. The various examples of ML applications are spam filtering, recommendations, predictive analytics and many more. AI and ML create smart systems by learning and making decisions using diverse data.

Pharmaceutical science is witnessing digitalization in all sectors. AI and ML are becoming an integral part of digital evolution in the pharmaceutical industry and experiencing significant shifts. The process of drug discovery, drug development, supply chain management and clinical trials have been revolutionized by the integration of AI and ML. It is also bringing the existing possibilities for progress for efficient drug discovery, predictive analytics and many more. The AI and ML enabled drug delivery systems will lead to faster, more efficient and more precise treatments.

1.2 Artificial Intelligence (AI)

AI is a branch of computer science that amalgamates statistics to exhibit the tasks of learning, decision-making, and prediction by utilizing algorithms or models. The flow of AI work is shown in Figure 1.1. The AI system clearly understands the problem and its scope. A better understanding of requirements and limitations leads to addressing the problem. Diverse sources (text, images, videos or sensors) are utilized to collect the data. The data is pre-processed for the purpose of cleaning and organisation. Data analysis can easily be performed using algorithms like decision trees or neural networks. These algorithms also help to spot the patterns of the data.

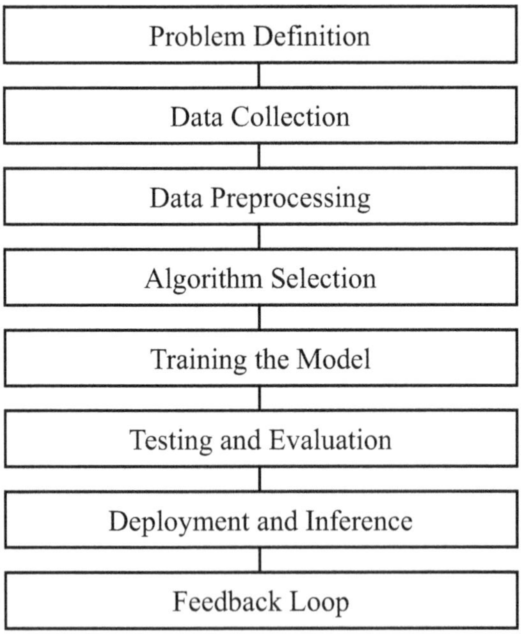

Figure 1.1 Flow of AI Work.

In order to minimise the prediction errors and to adjust the different parameters, the model is trained using the labelled data. The performance of the model can be evaluated using different sets of data, which also ensures the model's validation. The validated model can be further utilized to make predictions on another set of data. The continues improvements of any predictive model are necessary; therefore, the feedback loop is included in the AI system. The improvement process adjusts the parameters based on user feedback and/or can re-train using a new set of data. This step ensures the enhancement of predictive analysis and the model is well adopted.

The common applications of AI and ML witnessed in daily life are:

- ***Amazon and Flipkart:*** The e-commerce platform utilizes AI and ML to make product recommendations that enhance different aspects of the shopping experience. It also includes website services and warehouse automation.
- ***AarogyaSetu:*** A mobile app developed during Corona Virus Disease 2019 (COVID-19), was launched by the Government of India (GoI). It assesses the risk of infection using Bluetooth technology (BT), algorithms and AI, which allow users to gauge their exposure to the virus based on interactions with others. This app is available in different eleven languages. It facilitates timely government interventions.
- ***Tesla:*** It incorporates AI into electric vehicles for automatic driving capabilities, enhancing features such as automatic braking, lane changing and parking. Additionally, it explores AI and robotics for further advancements.
- ***Google Maps:*** It integrates AI to optimize routes for commuting, using algorithms to determine the best mode of transportation (car, foot, bike, bus, train) based on road information.
- ***Alexa:*** It is a virtual assistant developed by Amazon. Alexa processes voice commands through its built-in microphones, sending them to cloud servers for analysis. Using advanced AI, it interprets the request, retrieves relevant information and executes.
- ***Siri:*** This digital assistant has been integrated into the iPhone Operating System (iOS) by Apple since 2011 and aids with tasks like setting reminders, making calls and many more.
- ***Cortana:*** It serves as a personal productivity assistant in Microsoft 365, reminding users about emails and facilitating voice commands for meetings.
- ***Snapchat:*** It integrates AI into its mobile app, offering users filters for photos and a chatbot for trivia, trip suggestions and gift ideas.
- ***Bixby:*** This virtual assistant, developed by Samsung (in 2018), assists with phone functions, smart home control, and item location and is accessible on galaxy devices and Samsung appliances.

- ***AlphaSense:*** It develops an AI-powered financial search engine for investment firms, utilizing linguistic search and natural language processing to analyze financial data, generate actionable reports and saving analyst's time.
- ***Liberty Mutual:*** Liberty Mutual has partnered with the Massachusetts Institute of Technology (MIT) of United States to research AI solutions for modernizing the insurance industry. The research focuses on topics like transparency in decision-making algorithms and speeding up insurance claims processing.
- ***PathAI:*** It uses the AI-powered technology for pathologists for improving the diagnostic accuracy and treatment by analyzing tissue samples.

AI and ML have become indispensable tools in the pharmaceutical sector, offering precise handling and efficient work processes. Across the globe, several companies are accepting the AI system to minimize errors and provide better results in the field of drug development. These tools empower Research and Development (R&D) departments to gain valuable insights and streamline regulatory compliance by automating paperwork procedures. The AI aids in predicting valid results across various stages of product development, it is also important to acknowledge the invaluable role of human intellect. Some examples of AI applications associated with the pharmaceutical sector are:

- The Benevolent Platform™ (integrating technology, processes and human expertise) developed by Benevolent is a versatile platform for faster drug discovery process. It includes technology tailored for discovery and precision workflows.
- AI and Deep Learning (DL) are being used by the United States (US) based company Atomwise for drug discovery to accelerate the research in the area of various medical challenges like Ebola and multiple sclerosis.
- AusculThing ACC software, developed by AusculThing Oy (Finland), assists healthcare providers in interpreting and evaluating heart sounds in adults and children using an electronic stethoscope. Its AI-based algorithm detects heart murmurs of any intensity and categorizes heart sounds into abnormal and normal groups. However, it is not a standalone diagnostic device and works best alongside a physician's expertise and patient data. The software operates as a mobile app compatible with the Thinklabs One electronic stethoscope, offering both acoustic and visual playback of heart sounds for examinations and education. The supporting clinical decisions by visual and acoustic representations, AusculThing ACC enhances healthcare providers' capabilities, serving as a

supplementary tool to traditional diagnostic methods in cardiac care, with the potential to transform healthcare delivery and patient outcomes.

Classification of AI

AI can be classified into several types based on various criteria, including functionality, capability and approach. The common classifications of AI are shown in Table 1.1.

Table 1.1 Classification of AI based on functionality, capability and approach.

Classification	Types	Description
Based on Ability	Narrow AI (NAI)	Basic-level AI excelling at specific tasks, lacking human-like understanding. Examples include spam filters, voice assistants and personalized algorithms.
	General AI (GAI)	Aims to mimic human-like intelligence, including reasoning, problem-solving and learning from experience. However, replicating human cognition remains challenging.
	Super AI (SAI)	Hypothetical AI surpasses human intelligence, capable of autonomous improvement. Raises ethical concerns and existential threats.
Based on Functionality	Reactive AI (RAI)	Operates using algorithms to discern patterns from data, generating results without retaining memory of past occurrences. Examples include spam filters and Deep Blue chess computers.
	Limited Memory AI (LAI)	Learns from past experiences while making real-time decisions, enhancing decision-making capabilities. Examples include self-driving cars and image recognition software.

Table 1.1 *Contd...*

Classification	Types	Description
	Theory-of-Mind AI (TMAI)	Aims to understand human emotions, beliefs and intentions, adapting responses accordingly. It represents a frontier yet to be fully realized.
	Self-Aware AI (SAAI)	Theoretical concept wherein machines possess consciousness and self-awareness, surpassing human intelligence. Raises profound ethical and philosophical questions.
Problem-Solving Approaches	Symbolic AI (SyAI)	Represents knowledge using symbols and rules, enabling reasoning tasks.
	Connectionist AI (CAI)	Utilizes interconnected nodes arranged in layers, inspired by the human brain, to learn and solve problems.
	Evolutionary AI (EAI)	Draws inspiration from natural selection, employing algorithms like genetic programming to evolve and improve over time.

1. **Types of AI based on Ability**

   Based on the ability, AI can be classified into three categories that are:

   A. **Narrow Artificial Intelligence (NAI):** The basic level of AI, which is generally referred to as weak AI. This type of AI lacks general intelligence or in other words lacks human-like understanding, however, able to perform specific tasks. This AI system can perform the task within the programmed parameters. The spam filtering of email and voice assistants like Apple Siri or Amazon Alexa are common examples. This AI system can be used to play the game like chess or to manage the system through antilock brakes or fuel injection. Google Search is also one of the examples of narrow AI.

   B. **General Artificial Intelligence (GAI):** The main aim of the general AI is to mimic human-like intelligence and this type of AI is beyond narrow AI. It is generally referred to as strong AI or deep

AI. The goal is to understand complex ideas, problem-solving and reasoning abilities and learning from experience. The replication of the human brain's power possesses significant challenges. Social intelligence and creativity are major challenges for general AI. The general AI will offer significant advantages due to its problem-solving capabilities and processing speed and it may be able to execute multiple tasks.

C. **Super Artificial Intelligence (SAI):** The SAI is a hypothetical level in which the machines or systems may outperform human beings. It is proposed to surpass the human intelligence. This AI will improve all aspects like scientific creativity, general knowledge and social intelligence. The main focus is to have broad cognitive capabilities with learning, reasoning and adaptation without specific programming. The capabilities of autonomous improvements will lead to enhancement in cognitive abilities. The question of ethical implications and control mechanisms is of major concern. The foremost fear of Super AI is that it may be harmful to humanity.

2. **Classification of AI based on Functionality**

A. **Reactive AI (RAI):** RAI represents one of the fundamental forms of AI. It works through the application of algorithms and statistical models to identify and use patterns within data to produce results. A typical example of reactive AI is spam filtering. Other notable examples include Netflix's recommendation system and IBM's Deep Blue chess computer. The latter achieved a milestone by defeating the reigning chess champion through real-time analysis of the chessboard, without the ability to remember previous moves.

B. **Limited Memory AI (LAI):** It represents the advancement over RAI, wherein systems or machines learn from past experiences to make real-time decisions. The decision-making compliances are enhanced by the experimental knowledge and accumulations of vast data. The examples include self-driving cars and image recognition software. Self-driving cars utilize data from past experiences in order to anticipate future events which leads to enhanced the reliability on road. Similarly, image recognition software improves its accuracy over time by learning from diverse images. LAI also plays a vital role in diagnosis and treatments by analysing patient data and providing more accurate assessments.

C. **Theory-of-Mind AI (TMAI):** This AI is proposed to possess the understanding of human emotions, beliefs and intentions. However, it is yet to be fully recognized. It will understand the motives behind the behaviour of human beings and accordingly adopts the response. This AI will able to learn from a few examples and make precise decisions.

D. **Self-Aware AI (SAAI):** It is presently a theoretical concept. The machine or system has emotions, consciousness self-awareness and will surpass human intelligence. However, SAAI is still to be realized practically. The ethical and philosophical questions regarding the nature of consciousness are major concerns including human relationships.

3. **Classification of AI based on approaches**

   Based on problem-solving approaches AI can be classified also into three main categories:

   A. **Symbolic AI (SyAI):** The SyAI is also known as rule-based AI. SyAI represents knowledge using symbols or rules and allows the systems to perform reasoning tasks.

   B. **Connectionist AI (CAI):** This AI is inspired by the human brain. CAI utilizes interconnected nodes to learn and solve the different problems by adjusting connection strengths.

   C. **Evolutionary AI (EAI):** The EAI draws inspiration from natural selection and employ genetic programming to evolve and improve over time. These approaches represent distinct methodologies employed in developing AI systems for various applications.

The General Artificial Intelligence (GAI) aims to mimic human-like intelligence, whereas the Narrow Artificial Intelligence (NAI) focuses on specific tasks and a hypothetical level of intelligence surpassing human capabilities is represented by Super Artificial Intelligence (SAI). AI includes a spectrum of functionalities, ranging from basic reactive systems to theoretical concepts like self-awareness. While Reactive AI (RAI) and Limited Memory AI (LAI) are currently in use across various domains, Theory-of-Mind AI (TMAI) and Self-Aware AI (SAAI) represent ambitious goals for future advancements in the field. These classifications are not mutually exclusive and AI systems often integrate elements from multiple approaches to achieve their goals.

1.3 Machine Learning (ML)

ML is recognized as a subset of AI, whereby models are developed through the training of ML algorithms by analyzing data, without requiring absolute programming. The four most essential types of problems to be answered with machine learning are:

(a) Prediction,

(b) Classification,

(c) Grouping and

(d) Reducing dimensionality

ML efficiently handles large datasets, revealing complex patterns beyond human capacity. It automates tasks, liberating humans for more important work and improves accuracy over time, particularly in spam detection and forecasting. ML is able to predict outcomes in various areas like disease diagnosis, weather and stock markets that learn independently from data. The learning process in ML involves various steps as shown in Figure 1.2.

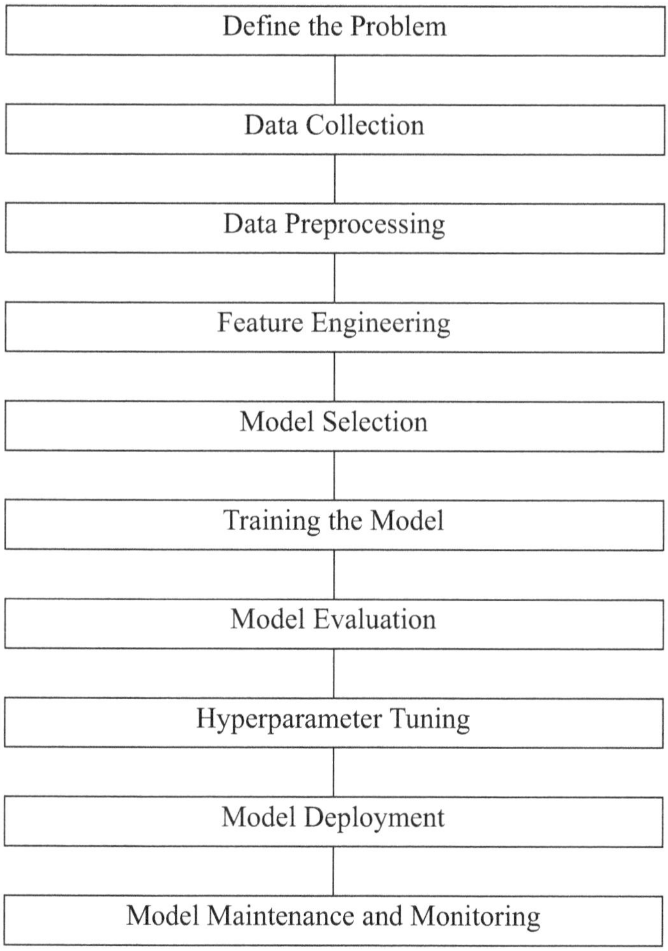

Figure 1.2 Flow of ML Work.

In the ML process, the initial step involves defining the problem to be addressed, understanding business or research objectives and specifying key requirements and constraints. Following this, relevant data is collected from various sources and pre-processed to ensure quality. Feature engineering is then employed to extract pertinent information and optimize model performance. Subsequently, an appropriate model is selected based on the problem's nature and dataset characteristics. This model is trained using optimized data and evaluated using appropriate metrics. Hyperparameters are tuned to enhance the model performance. Upon satisfactory evaluation, the model is deployed into production for predictions, requiring ongoing maintenance and monitoring to ensure continued effectiveness and adaptation to changing data distributions. ML can be broadly classified into three main types based on the nature of the learning process and the type of data, as shown in Table 1.2.

Table 1.2 Classification of ML.

Type of Machine Learning	Description
Supervised Learning (SL)	Trained on labeled data, pairs to predict outputs for new data. Tasks include regression (continuous output prediction) and classification (discrete label prediction).
Unsupervised Learning (UL)	Given unlabeled data, aims to find hidden patterns. Tasks include clustering (grouping similar data points) and dimensionality reduction (reducing features while retaining important information).
Semi-supervised Learning (SSL)	Utilizes both labeled and unlabeled data, improving learning algorithm performance. Approaches include self-training (iteratively adding pseudo-labeled unlabeled instances), co-training (multiple models exchange labels) and graph-based methods (label propagation based on graph structure).
Reinforcement Learning (RL)	Learned by interacting with an environment and optimizing actions to maximize cumulative rewards. Involves exploration (trying new actions) versus exploitation (leveraging known actions for rewards).

1. **Supervised Learning (SL):** SL requires labeled input and output data during the training phase. It relies on human supervision to guide the learning process. The goal is typically to predict outcomes based on available data, which can involve either regression (for example predicting continuous values, like house prices) or classification (for example predicting discrete labels or categories, such as spam or non-spam emails). The challenges include the need for high-quality labeled data and appropriate model selection. Regression (predicting continuous values) and classification (predicting discrete labels or categories) are the most common tasks.
2. **Unsupervised Learning (UL):** It deals entirely with raw data and no labels are provided. Rather, the algorithm finds hidden patterns in it. This approach is used for types of results that are not predetermined against target variables, usually applied to similar types of data. Techniques of dimensionality reduction such as Principal Component Analysis (PCA) reduce a dataset while retaining important patterns. While clustering, such as K-means clustering, groups the similar data points together.
3. **Semi-Supervised Learning (SSL):** It falls between supervised (SL) and unsupervised learning (UL). Mixing labeled and unlabeled data is used for training, where the labeled dataset is relatively small and the unlabeled one is large. SSL based applied techniques include self-training, co-training and graph-based methods. For example, image classification may use a small set of labeled images that can be combined with a larger set of unlabeled images to create a more accurate model.
4. **Reinforcement Learning (RL):** The basic idea behind RL is to learn from the environment, like human beings. This allows the algorithm to learn through interactions with the environment. The actions taken by the algorithm affect the environment, which in turn provides feedback to the algorithm in the form of rewards or punishments. This feedback guides the algorithm in learning the policy to make decisions. Examples include robots learning to perform tasks like walking or cleaning and systems like DeepMind's AlphaGo which learned to play games through RL. In RL, there is a delicate balance between exploration, where an individual or organisation tries new actions and exploitation, in which it exploits known actions for immediate rewards.

1.4 Deep Learning (DL)

DL is a subdomain of ML, a branch of AI that uses algorithms known as Artificial Neural Networks (ANNs). ANNs are inspired by the neural networks of the human brain. These algorithms are structured in layers, creating Deep Neural Networks (DNNs), where each layer extracts progressively more abstract features from the data. DL can learn all the features from raw data, removing the need for manual feature engineering. With large sets of labeled data and powerful computing, DL models are able to learn directly from beginning to end, and further improve as they go. DL finds application in diverse areas such as image recognition, speech recognition, natural language processing, drug discovery, recommendation systems, autonomous driving and many more. In addition, DLs are able to adapt to different amounts of data and computing power, making them versatile. For example, a class of DLs known as convolutional neural networks can work well for image analysis. This allows accurate segmentation of organs and tissues from images obtained through computed tomography (CT), which also allows accurate measurements of their anatomy to be taken and assists in surgical planning. Furthermore, DL algorithms are able to detect many more abnormalities associated with tumors or lesions through CT scans. Therefore, this supports radiologists to detect and diagnose dangerous diseases like cancer at an early stage. The relationship between AI, ML and DL is illustrated in Figure 1.3.

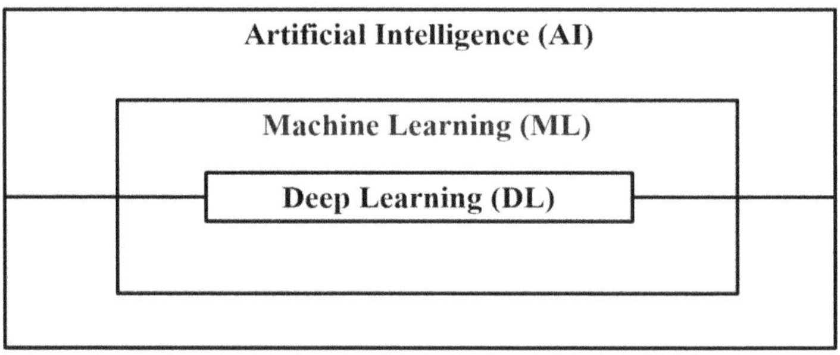

Figure 1.3 Relationship between AI, ML and DL.

The AI, ML and DL have inherent characteristics and applications:

- AI primarily focus on systems which can performs tasks associated with human intelligence, including language understanding, problem solving, pattern recognition and experimental learning and many more. The subfields of AI are natural language processing, computer vision and robotics.
- The subset of AI is the ML, which deals with development of algorithms and methodologies. The main feature of ML is to make

predictions or decisions without being programmed. The ML algorithms learn from data (pattern & correlation) and make informed decision/ predictions.

- The DL is a subset of ML, which works in the similar way to the neural network of human brain. The Artificial Neural Network (ANN) is composed of layers filled with interconnected nodes called neurons. The impact is processed in stages, which mirror the coordinated work of neurons in human brain. The processing in steps is required for operation of ANN & biological neural networks.

DL excels at many complex tasks, such as image recognition, speech understanding, natural language (NL) processing and many more. Its performance is particularly impressive when a wealth of data is available for training these systems. However, training DL models can be quite resource-intensive, especially for large-scale projects with the advancements of supporting technology such as Tensor Processing Units (TPUs) and Graphics Processing Units (GPUs) as well as user-friendly software frameworks such as TensorFlow and PyTorch. DL algorithms have become more accessible and powerful tools, allowing their widespread use in a variety of fields, including pharmaceutical sciences.

1.5 Neural Network (NN)

NN is a widely used form of AI/ML that excels in categorization applications. They have often been loosely compared to how neurons in the brain process the signals. NN serves as a computational model inspired by the structure and functioning of the human brain's interconnected network of neurons, mimicking the way these biological neurons transmit and process information. NNs are structured in a specific way, consisting of at least three primary layers:

- The network receives information and serves as primary data entry point is act as input layer.
- The hidden layer is located between the input and output layers. It is essential for processing. It extracts patterns and runs internal calculations on the supplied data. Multiple hidden layers improve the network's ability to understand and learn from complex data.
- The output layer generates the final output depending on the computations from the hidden layers. It transforms internal processing into understandable and useful results.

Backpropagation is a neural network training algorithm that modifies weights and biases based on the difference between predicted and actual outputs. The chain rule of calculus governs it and it is an essential component of most neural network training algorithms.

Artificial Neural Networks (ANNs)

ANNs are subtypes of NNs that are used for pattern recognition, classification, regression and other ML tasks. ANNs are composed of interconnected nodes called artificial neurons (ANs). These artificial neurons are inspired by biological neurons found in the human brain. Neurons receive inputs from other neurons and send outputs. The weight is assigned to connections between neurons. These weights determine the strength of the signal transmitted from one neuron to another. The higher the weight, the stronger the signal. The learning process for ANNs involves changing the weights of the connections linking the neurons and is referred to as training. This starts training with some given data set and then tries to learn the patterns in that data. The weights of the connections are adjusted according to how well the network performs on the training data. After training, this network can be used to predict or classify new data.

1.6 Data Types and Resources

Data is the currency of the current digital age. Data is the prior information saved in numerous forms, such as numbers, text, images, videos and many more. Data can be structured in databases, but it can also be unstructured, such as social media posts. It is used for decision-making and to understand things in science, business and daily life. Data forms a central role in AI and ML, as it is the fuel that keeps them running—continually learning and making decisions. AI and ML success is probably not possible and the without good quality data, which assists an AI or ML model in making highly precise decisions by reducing errors and enhancing the predictive results. High-quality data makes training better in capturing important patterns. Effective patterns cannot be identified unless there is enough high-quality data for the AI and ML systems to make proper, accurate predictions and provide valuable insights. For example, in image recognition, a neural network needs access to a large dataset of labeled images to learn how to accurately labeled new images it encounters. Without this data, the AI system would not be able to distinguish between different objects or recognize patterns within them. In the context of AI and ML, data and resources play crucial roles in model development, training and deployment. Some important data forms used in the pharmaceutical sector are:

- **Categorical Data:** The data that fits into categories is known as categorised data. It doesn't consist of numerical values but consists of distinct categories/groups representing qualities or classifications. The two main types of categorical data are:
    - Nominal data, which has no inherent order (e.g., hair colour, blood group type).

  - Ordinal data, which has a specific ranking (e.g., satisfaction ratings, education level).

  Analyzing the categorical data helps to identify trends and relationships between the groups.

- **Quantitative and numerical data**: This is all about numbers and measurements. This kind of data tells us how much or how many of something there is? There are two main types:
  - Discrete Data: This type consists of whole numbers, like counts. For example, the number of students in a class or the number of books on a shelf.
  - Continuous Data: This type can be any value within a range. For example, height, weight, temperature, or time.

  Numerical data can be either continuous or discontinuous. Continuous data is data that can take any value within a range, while discrete is data with particular values. Analyzing this data requires methods like averages and graphs in statistics to see trends and then make decisions based on how things are going. Examples are the number of website visitors per day and the height of students in the class. Therefore, numbers that can be counted or measured at any time are classified as quantitative and numerical data.

- **Chemical data**: This type of data includes information regarding chemical compounds, including their molecular structures, properties, and interactions. Chemical data is quantitative and numerical which mainly focuses on the properties, composition and structure of chemicals. Chemical data may be as simple as molecular and structural formulas, chemical and physical property data, spectral data from spectroscopy and many more. All such data is very important in a wide array of areas like chemical research and engineering, environmental science, medicine and many more. The most common sources that provide access to chemical data are the chemical databases PubChem and ChemSpider, scientific literature and Safety Data Sheets (SDSs), which include information on the hazards of chemicals and how to handle them.

  In the context of AI/ML, it is utilized for analyzing chemical datasets to aid in drug discovery and design, involving predictive modelling for potential drug candidates and molecular docking algorithms for assessing interactions with target proteins.

- **Clinical data (CD):** CD is information about patients data collected in healthcare settings. It includes patient demographics, vital signs or symptoms, laboratory results, imaging studies, medication use, symptoms and diagnoses, treatment information and others. There are two main types of clinical data:

- o Prospective data: This data is collected as part of a planned study, such as a clinical trial.
- o Retrospective data: This data is collected from existing medical records.

Clinical data play a significant role in the modern healthcare sector. Adequate collection, analysis and utilization of clinical data enhance the quality of care given to patients by healthcare providers.

- **Imaging data (ID):** ID is a special type of clinical data that uses visual representations related to the internal part of the human body. ID including medical images from modalities such as X-ray, magnetic resonance imaging (MRI) and CT scans, allows disease detection, progression and AI/ML-assisted diagnosis. It provides important information on body structures, helping health professionals to diagnose and monitor many diseases. Imaging data are stored in digital formats and because of their concentration in visual forms expressing the body, they require specialized methods of analysis.
- **Sensor Data (SD):** SD data is collected by sensors in the environment, whether it is health or manufacturing. The sensors detect physical, chemical, or biological phenomena. They are applied for monitoring weather, activity tracking, or process optimization, among other uses. Examples include temperature sensors, pressure sensors, motion sensors and many more. In pharmaceutical manufacturing, a good number of sensor types are involved in acquiring the data, from simple wearables to state-of-the-art biosensors. These in turn help AI in real-time monitoring of patients for the effectiveness of drugs and predictability of treatment plans. For example, LifeBEAM Smart Helmets integrate biometric sensors for fitness monitoring during sports that provide real-time information on heart rate and performance.

In the pharmaceutical sector, both labeled and unlabeled data are very important to use smart computer technologies. The difference between labeled and unlabeled data is shown in Table 1.3. Labeled Data (LD) is good for training models in supervised learning such as predicting drug efficacy or diagnosing diseases from medical scans. Unlabeled Data (UD) is useful in unsupervised learning which has the capability of finding hidden patterns in patient data for the discovery of new drugs or mechanisms of disease. Both labeled and unlabeled data drive great progress in the pharmaceutical sector.

Table 1.3 Difference between Labeled and Unlabeled Data.

Labeled Data	Unlabeled Data
Tagged with specific categories or labels.	Lacks specific tags or categories.
Patient records with outcomes like drug effectiveness.	Patient information without specific drug response labels.
Training supervised learning models.	Utilized for unsupervised learning tasks.
Predicting drug efficacy and disease diagnosis.	Identifying new drug targets and understanding disease mechanisms.
Efficient for tasks requiring specific outcomes.	Powerful for revealing hidden patterns and associations.
Analysed through supervised learning algorithms.	Analysed using unsupervised learning techniques.
May be more limited and specific.	Tends to be more abundant but requires advanced analysis.
More structured and straightforward.	Can be more complex and varied.
Crucial for tasks requiring predefined outcomes.	Essential for discovering new patterns or relationships.
Directly contributes to decision-making processes.	Indirectly informs research directions and strategy.

1.7 Data Management

Data management involves the effective management of an organization's data through practices, tools and techniques. In modern times, efficient management of data has become very important during the continuous creation and storage of information. The primary objectives of data management include availability of data to authorised end-users, maintaining data quality through accuracy and consistency, protecting data through security measures, enforcing privacy principles and promulgating responsible data governance policies and procedures. Effective data management creates many benefits such as better decision-making, improved operational efficiency, reduced costs, increased regulatory compliance and improved customer experience. Efficient management of data is the most important element of organizational data management. It covers the entire activities from creation or acquisition of data to storage, usage and finally destruction. In Figure 1.4, the entire data management process including data collection, storage, processing, analysis and dissemination has been illustrated.

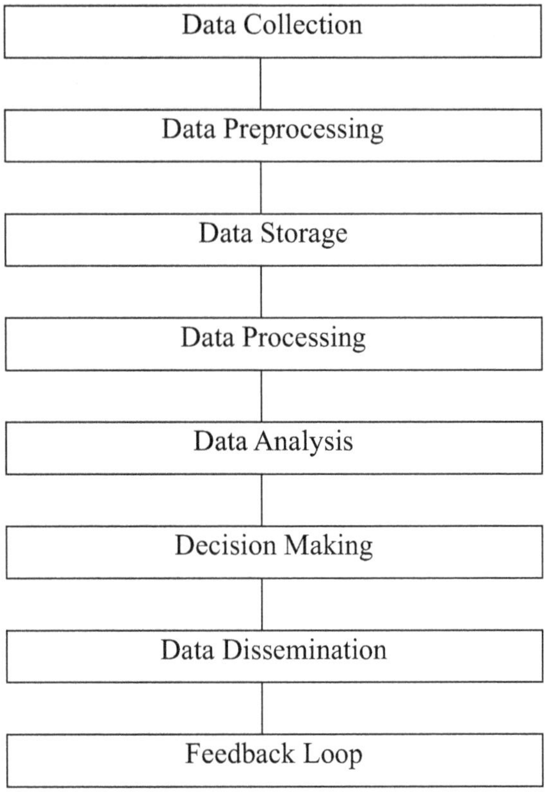

Figure 1.4 Data Management Process.

Initially, for data collection, sources of other data such as databases, application programming interfaces, sensors and other forms are identified. The raw data is gathered from these sources. After that, data preprocessing is done where the data is cleaned to remove duplicates, fix errors and handle missing values, also called Data Pruning (DP). DP refers to the removal of irrelevant or unnecessary data from the dataset. DP in AI/ML makes model trains more efficient by removing noisy or misleading data and preprocessing them to create a more efficient model. DP optimizes query performance and analyzes it to remove irrelevant data, so that one can achieve quick queries to the database. Data may be normalized or standardized to prepare it for analysis. Appropriate storage solutions, such as databases, data lakes, or cloud storage, are in place to ensure data security and compliance with regulations such as the Digital Personal Data Protection Act, 2023 in India and the General Data Protection Regulation (GDPR) in Europe. It is necessary to comply with all applicable regulations to protect against the misuse of data across the world.

The computations and calculations are performed on the data in data processing phase (may include aggregation or summarization). In this phase, the transformation of data or filter is also applied. During the data analysis phase, for the purpose of meaningful insights of data, the different statistical methods & ML algorithms are utilized. The data can be presented in the form of graph or charts for better understanding. The interpretation of the results of analysis are performed in the decision making phase and on the basis of insights gained, the action/strategies are taken and planned further. The reports thus generated can also be presented/shown to the stakeholders. The utmost care should be taken with regard to data security and privacy along with ease of access of information. The inputs from stakeholders' regarding effective data management can be supported during the phase of feedback loop. The feedback plays a vital role in the improvement and optimization of the process.

The quality, analysis and decisions can easily be improved by the AI technology, which aid in systematic management of an organization's data. The diverse technical approaches can be well adopted during collection, organization, storage and secure use of data. The main aim is to ensure data accuracy, accessibility, security and compliance in order to make final decision and to meet the regulatory compliances.

The various ways to improve the data management are:

- Data Cleaning: The detection and fixing of errors, finding inconsistencies and duplication in datasets can be performed by AI system through data cleaning. It ensures data accuracy and reliability for decision-making.
- Data Noise Reduction/Data Pruning (DP): The useful information can be separated from irrelevant data. The time and resources can be saved by the organization by AI technologies.
- Missing Data: The correction and statistical modeling are effective in imputing missing data by AI methods. The significant increase in data accuracy and usefulness and reduction of negative impacts on results is feasible.
- Spotting Trends: In this step the correlations, trends and hidden patterns within large datasets can be detected by AI powered analytical tools. This capability helps the organizations to predict market trends and make proactive decisions.

1.8 History of AI and ML in the Pharmaceutical and Healthcare Sector

The integration of AI and ML in the pharmaceutical and healthcare sectors has a long history marked by steady growth which has gained significant momentum in recent years. These technologies have revolutionized various aspects of pharmaceutical research, drug discovery and healthcare delivery. Some of the key developments related to AI and ML in pharmaceuticals and healthcare are highlighted in Table 1.4.

Table 1.4 Historical Milestone of AI and ML in Pharmaceutical and Healthcare.

Year	Description
1943	Warren McCulloch and Walter Pitts developed the first computational model of a neuron in their paper "*A Logical Calculus of the Ideas Immanent in Nervous Activity.*" They aimed to understand how the brain generates complex patterns through interconnected basic cells.
1950	The 'Turing Test' was proposed by Alan Turing, which is a method for evaluating the intelligence of machines by engaging them in natural language conversations. AI and ML techniques are widely used in both the process of passing the test and assessing its outcomes.
1956	John McCarthy Coined the term "artificial intelligence". In early 1956, Herbert Simon announced the invention of a "thinking machine" called the Logic Theorist, co-created with Al Newell. This program could prove theorems in propositional logic, solving 38 out of 52 theorems in '*Principia Mathematica*' (PM). It was among the first programs to simulate human problem-solving abilities, influencing the emerging field of information-processing psychology in the late 1950s.
1966	ELIZA: Early chatbot created by Joseph Weizenbaum which used pattern matching for conversations, pioneering AI in chatbots.
1966-1972	Shakey, the "*first electronic person*" (Robot) was developed. Shakey was developed at Stanford Research Institute (United States) marking the first mobile robot capable of interpreting complex instructions. It represented a significant advancement in robotics and AI.
1971	Rutgers University (United States) received funding for a pilot research resource on computers in biomedicine. The resource supported research on problem-solving in life sciences and psychology, as well as pattern recognition models for clinical decisions.

Table 1.4 *Contd...*

Year	Description
1972	MYCIN is an early expert system developed by Stanford University (United States) scientists to demonstrate expert-level performance in the diagnosis and treatment of blood infections through rule-based reasoning. Despite its limitations, such as a small knowledge base and inability to learn from new data, MYCIN pioneered the use of expert systems in real-world problem-solving, inspiring further development in AI for healthcare.
1973	Stanford University (United States) Medical Experimental – AI in Medicine (SUMEX-AIM), received funding as an inter-university resource. SUMEX-AIM facilitated collaboration among researchers from Stanford (United States), Rutgers (United States), Pittsburgh (United States), and Tufts University with Harvard University (United States) and Massachusetts Institute of Technology (United States) which is known as TuftsHarvard-MIT (due cross registration agreements between TuftsHarvard-MIT).
1975	The first National Institutes of Health (NIH) (United states) -sponsored Artificial Intelligence in Medicine (AIM) workshop was held.
1980	EMYCIN provides a blueprint for building expert systems, based on MYCIN (without medical knowledge). Developers can add their own rules, making it useful in different areas. Although not directly diagnosing diseases, EMYCIN opened the way for the creation of similar programs in different domains.
1981	Computer-aided drug design (CADD) revolutionized compound characterization in drug discovery. Unlike High throughput screening (HTS), it needs minimal compound design or prior knowledge but can yield multiple promising hit compounds.
1986	DXplain, developed by the University of Massachusetts (United States), generates a differential diagnosis using inputted symptoms. It also acts as an electronic medical textbook, offering detailed disease descriptions and references. Initially covering around 500 diseases, it has expanded to over 2400 diseases. This, along with renewed interest in machine learning in the late 1990s, laid the groundwork for the modern era of artificial intelligence in medicine.
2000	The term "Deep Learning" (DL) has gained popularity.

Table 1.4 *Contd...*

Year	Description
2007	IBM's Watson, an open-domain question-answering system, triumphed over human competitors on the TV game shown Jeopardy!
2011	DeepQA is an advanced question-answering system developed by IBM. DeepQA uses advanced NLP, ML and information retrieval techniques to understand and answer questions asked in natural language.
2011	AI trials in gastroenterology was performed.
2011-2017	Mainstream consumer products like Apple's Siri (2011) and Amazon's Alexa (2014) demonstrate the integration of NLP into virtual assistants (based on ELIZA). In healthcare, NLP-powered chatbots have made significant progress. o Pharmabot, introduced in 2015 offers tailored medication education for pediatric patients and parents. o Mandy, developed in 2017 automates patient intake processes in primary care, improving efficiency and patient experiences through conversational interfaces.
2016	Pfizer teams up with IBM Watson Health to fast-track immuno-oncology research using AI.
2022	Insilico Medicine a company from Hong Kong, has developed a drug called INS018_055 using AI. INS018_055 is the first fully AI-derived drug to enter clinical trials.
2023	Merck has launched AIDDISON™, a new software platform. It bridges the gap between virtual molecule design and real-world manufacturability, using Synthia™ retrosynthesis API integration.

In the 21st century, AI and ML have transformed the pharmaceutical sector by making drug discovery faster, tailoring treatments for individuals, improving clinical trials, ensuring safer medications and engaging patients more effectively. These technologies are reshaping how medicines are developed and used, ultimately benefiting patients worldwide. AI and ML are growing in the pharmaceutical industry, especially in drug development and biomedical research. By 2025, most of the healthcare organizations worldwide are expected to use AI and ML technology.

1.9 Opportunities and Challenges of AI and ML in Pharmaceutical Sciences

AI and ML are changing the way various products and services are discovered and developed in the pharmaceutical industry. Imagine AI as a super-smart assistant helps the scientists to find new treatments faster and with fewer side effects. It does this by analyzing huge amounts of biological data to pinpoint potential targets for new drugs, like certain proteins or genes related to diseases. With AI and ML help, scientists can design new medications more efficiently, making the whole process smoother. Some opportunities associated with AI and ML are shown in Table 1.5.

Table 1.5 Opportunities Associated with AI and ML in Pharmaceutical Sciences.

Opportunity	Description
Drug Discovery and Development	New drugs can be found faster with AI and ML by analyzing big data. For example, Atomwise uses AI to discover new drugs quickly.
Personalized Medicine	Treatments can be personalized based on patient characteristics using AI and ML. For example, IBM Watson for Oncology suggests personalized cancer treatments.
Predictive Analytics in Clinical Trials	Clinical trials become more efficient with AI and ML predicting patient responses. For example, Owkin's platform predicts treatment outcomes in trials.
Drug Repurposing	AI and ML find new uses for existing drugs. For example, BenevolentAI discovers new applications for drugs efficiently.
Precision Drug Manufacturing	Drug manufacturing is improved using AI and ML to control production variables.
Drug Safety and Pharmacovigilance	AI and ML monitor drug safety using real-world data. Pfizer uses AI to monitor drug safety effectively.
Virtual Drug Screening	AI and ML screen compounds quickly for potential drugs. Insilico methods uses AI for rapid drug screening.
Disease Diagnosis and Prognosis	AI and ML aid in diagnosing diseases and predicting outcomes. Google's DeepMind Health helps in diagnosing eye diseases early.

AI and ML are not just helpful in laboratories but also make clinical trials safer for participants by predicting potential risks from new drugs. In addition, it can even find new uses for existing medications, helping to treat more diseases. When it's time to test new drugs on people, AI makes it easier to find the right volunteers by sorting through their health records. After a drug is approved, AI and ML keep working behind the scenes, monitoring how well it works and is safe for real patients. It also helps drug companies to make medicines faster and cheaper while making sure that they must meet quality standards. When the doctors need to prescribe medications, AI helps them choose the best and safest ones for each patient.

Despite the myriad benefits that AI and ML bring to healthcare, they also present significant challenges. A major issue is managing the large amounts of health information or data (including structured and unstructured data) used by AI systems. The Health Information Management (HIM) plays an important role, acting as custodian of health care data. HIM ensures its accuracy, security and appropriate use. The AI and ML are becoming more common and the HIM managers need to learn new skills to adapt to the changing landscape & run operations efficiently. The integration of AI and machine learning in pharmaceutical sciences presents challenges. Some challenges of AI and ML associated with the pharmaceutical sector are shown in Table 1.6.

Table 1.6 Challenges Associated with AI and ML in Pharmaceutical Sciences.

Challenges	Description
Data Quality and Quantity	In pharmaceutical sciences, AI and ML struggle when data is insufficient or low-quality, affecting accuracy. For example, incomplete patient records impact predictive models.
Interpretability of AI Models	Understanding AI decisions is vital. However, many models may lack clarity at a certain level.
Regulatory Compliance and Validation	Adhering to regulatory guidelines is tough for AI in pharmaceuticals. For example, validating AI for clinical decision support demands extensive testing.
Integration with Existing Systems	Blending AI into current pharmaceutical systems faces hurdles due to compatibility issues and resistance. Implementing AI in drug discovery might need substantial changes.
Ethical and Privacy Concerns	Key concerns include patient data security and fairness in AI/ML-based decision-making. Implementing AI in patient data analysis requires many obligations regarding ethics and privacy.
Computational Resource Requirements	AI in pharmaceuticals demands significant computational power, any may be costly. Training Deep Learning models for drug discovery might need specialized hardware and resources.
Collaboration and Skill Gap	Effective use of AI needs collaboration between experts and data scientists. Bridging this gap fosters better solutions, like AI-driven drug discovery.
Robustness and Generalization Capability	AI must perform reliably across various datasets and scenarios. Overfitting to specific data or failing to generalize can undermine effectiveness.

AI systems must provide comprehensive, accurate and reliable data to predict outcomes accurately. The quality and governance of this data is critical in delivering reliable results while dealing with the associated legal, ethical and regulatory issues. Problems of healthcare data consumption, complex logistics and the high initial cost of setting up and maintaining AI infrastructure are significant obstacles in the adoption of AI for the pharmaceutical industry.

AI systems lack human intelligence when attempting to mimic human behaviour. Therefore, in areas where the required data is not available within the database, human input plays an extremely important role, especially in areas like drug development and supply chain management. As the AI systems cannot learn through experience, they must be constantly updated and maintained to remain effective and relevant over time. More pharmaceutically relevant integration of AI and ML into pharmaceutical practices protects patient privacy and gains regulatory approval. The AI systems can process large amounts of healthcare data and it is important to protect sensitive patient information from cyber threats. Obtaining regulatory approval for AI-powered procedures in clinical studies requires navigating complex legal frameworks and uncertain data sharing and privacy rules in many jurisdictions.

1.10 Digital Technology Trends in the Pharmaceutical Industry

Digital technologies are rapidly changing the pharmaceutical industry. These technologies are constantly used to accelerate drug discovery and development, improve clinical trial efficiency and deliver drugs on a more personalized basis. Table 1.7 shows some of the digital technology trends associated with the pharmaceutical sector.

Table 1.7 Digital Technology Trends.

Technology	Description
Mobile Health (mHealth)	Mobile apps, SMS and other mobile technologies are used for health-related purposes such as remote monitoring, medication reminders and health education.
Telemedicine/ Telehealth	Virtual consultations, remote monitoring and telehealth platforms enable remote access to healthcare services, improving accessibility and reducing the need for in-person visits.
Electronic Health Records (EHR)	Digital systems for storing, managing and sharing patients' health information securely among healthcare providers, facilitating better coordination of care and reducing medical errors.

Table 1.7 *Contd...*

Technology	Description
Wearable Devices	Devices worn by individuals to track health metrics like heart rate, activity levels and sleep patterns, providing real-time data for personalized health management.
Health Analytics and Artificial Intelligence (AI)	Advanced analytics and insights from data can be used to make clinical decisions, disease prevention and plan healthcare. It also uses AI-enabled tools and algorithms to analyze health data for clinical support, patient outcome prediction and task automation to ensure effective healthcare delivery.
Blockchain Technology	Distributed ledger technology ensures secure and transparent management of healthcare data, supporting applications like supply chain management and identity management.
Digital Therapeutics (DTx)	Software-based interventions for preventing, managing, or treating medical conditions, complement traditional medical treatments with digital solutions.

The use of AI and ML in healthcare is revolutionizing various processes, including drug target identification and patient response prediction. These methods will be complemented by big data analytics, which extract valuable insights from massive amounts of data. Cloud computing enables secure data storage and collaboration across different locations. The Internet of Medical Things (IoMT) and Digital Therapeutics (DTx) are developing new treatment options and increasing patient monitoring and treatment. Nonetheless, blockchain technology ensures the integrity of clinical trial data and allows tracing the origin of a drug, bringing a new level of security and transparency to healthcare.

Digital Health Technologies (DHT) include a number of cutting-edge tools designed to improve care delivery and patient outcomes. These include mobile health (mHealth) applications, telemedicine, electronic health records (EHR), wearable devices, health analytics, AI/ML-based products and services and many more. At its core, these technologies enable healthcare providers to deliver efficient, personalized and proactive care, reshaping the way care is delivered to the patients. DHTs provide benefits when using healthcare services, such as remote access, better care coordination through EHRs and more recently, personalised health management through wearable devices, IoT-based devices, AI algorithms and others.

These technologies simplify research and accelerate drug discovery and development. Predictive modelling brings personalized treatments closer, ensuring tailored solutions for patients. The collaboration between human knowledge and AI and ML algorithms unlocks revolutionary breakthroughs in different aspects of the pharmaceutical sector. Embracing these advancements promises a brighter future for pharmaceuticals, which ultimately improve healthcare outcomes and enhance Quality Of Life (QOL) worldwide.

Proposed Questions

Long Answer Type Questions (10 Marks Each)

1. How are AI and ML being integrated into pharmaceutical sciences?
2. What are the benefits of using AI and ML in pharmaceutical research?
3. Define Artificial intelligence (AI) and machine Learning (ML). Discuss their key concepts as well as components in the context of the pharmaceutical sector.
4. What challenges and opportunities are associated with implementing AI and ML in the pharmaceutical sector?
5. Describe the key milestones in the history of AI and ML associated with the pharmaceutical industry.
6. What future developments can be expected in AI and ML applications within pharmaceutical sciences? Discuss briefly.
7. Describe digital technology trends in the pharmaceutical industry.
8. How do AI and ML help us in everyday life? How these technologies are making things easier for us?
9. What are the different types of data used in AI and ML?. Where can the researchers and developers find these resources to train the models effectively?
10. How do any organizations handle data governance and compliance as part of the data management process?

Short Answer Type Questions (5 Marks Each)

1. What are some practical applications of AI and ML in the pharmaceutical sector?
2. What are the some ways by which AI and ML helps to keep the medicines safe?
3. What is the difference between labeled and unlabeled data in AI and ML?
4. How are unlabeled data used in machine learning?

5. Write a short note on the classification of AI.
6. Give a note on the classification of ML.
7. How do companies collect and utilize data to improve their AI-powered products and services?

Very Short Questions (1 Mark)

1. Who is known as the "Father of AI"?
2. What is Artificial Intelligence (AI)?
3. What is Machine Learning (Ml)?
4. What are some common uses of AI?
5. How does AI make tasks easier?
6. Why is data important in ML?
7. How does ML help predict outcomes?
8. How do AI-powered chatbots improve business operations?
9. How do AI chatbots help patients?
10. What is a common challenge in implementing AI in healthcare systems?

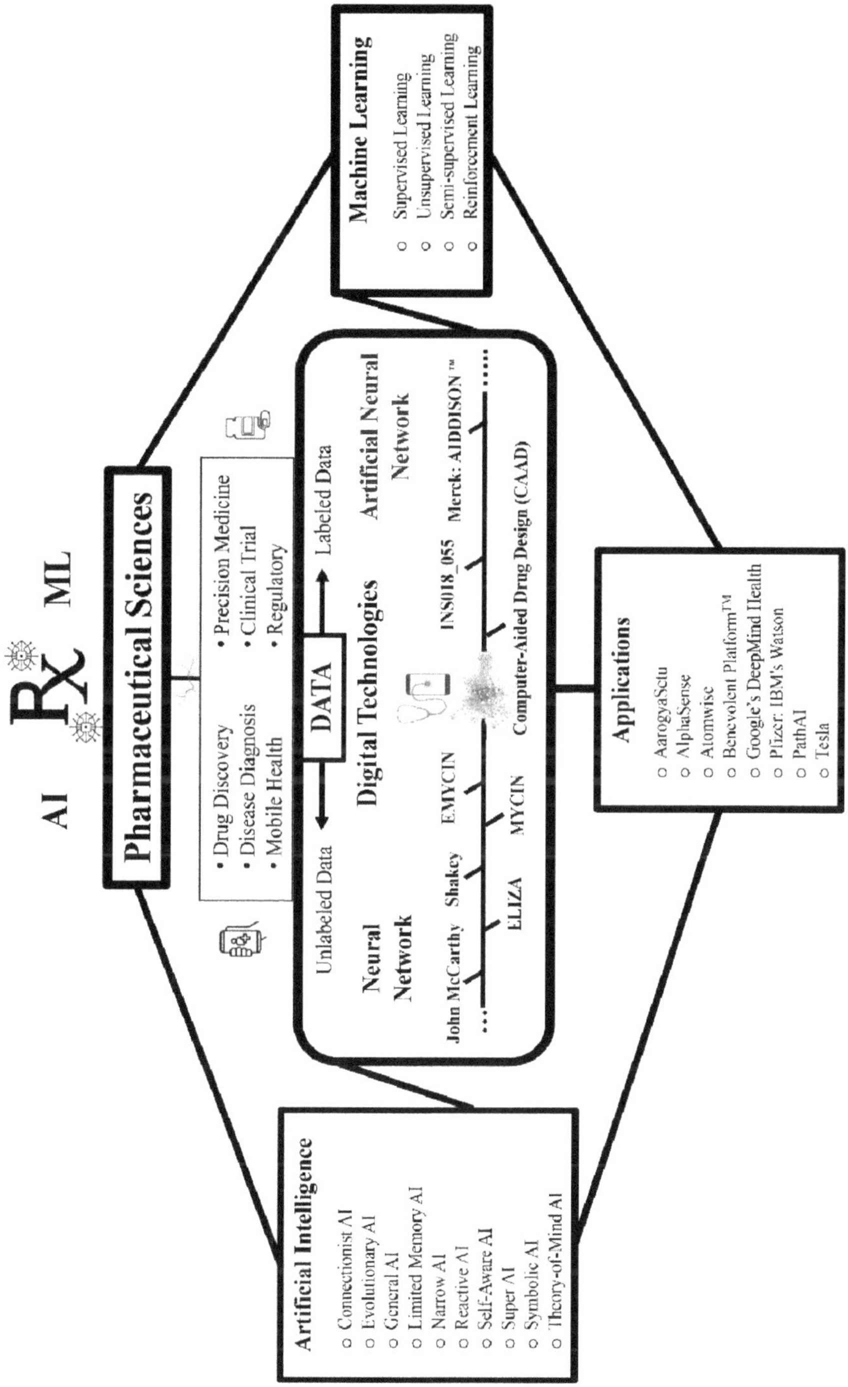
AI Rx ML
Pharmaceutical Sciences
• Drug Discovery
• Disease Diagnosis
• Mobile Health
• Precision Medicine
• Clinical Trial
• Regulatory
Unlabeled Data
DATA
Labeled Data
Neural Network
Digital Technologies
Artificial Neural Network
John McCarthy
Shakey
EMYCIN
INS018_055
Merck: AIDDISON™
ELIZA
MYCIN
Computer-Aided Drug Design (CAAD)
Artificial Intelligence
Connectionist AI
Evolutionary AI
General AI
Limited Memory AI
Narrow AI
Reactive AI
Self-Aware AI
Super AI
Symbolic AI
Theory-of-Mind AI
Applications
AarogyaSetu
AlphaSense
Atomwise
Benevolent Platform™
Google's DeepMind Health
Pfizer: IBM's Watson
PathAI
Tesla
Machine Learning
Supervised Learning
Unsupervised Learning
Semi-supervised Learning
Reinforcement Learning

CHAPTER 2

AI and ML in Pharmaceutical Research and Development

2.1 Introduction

In recent years, the landscape of pharmaceutical Research and Development (R&D) has witnessed significant transformation due to the emergence of game-changing technologies like Artificial Intelligence (AI) and Machine Learning (ML). These changes are driving progress, creating new ways while leaving old ones behind. AI and ML are everywhere, enhancing various kinds of products in the market. In simple terms, AI is like an intelligent machine that can think and solve problems like humans. At the same time, ML is a part of AI that focuses on creating more innovative machines using algorithms without human intervention. In recent years, AI and ML are rapidly changing the pharmaceutical R & D landscape. The discovery process for medicinal products takes many years and most molecules do not work as desired, leading to high costs and risks. AI has great potential to assist by analysing massive amounts of data and identifying the best target sites for new drugs, like finding the correct key for the lock. Companies are now emphasising the 4P approach with AI and ML, which are mentioned below:

- Predictive: AI and ML analysis of patient data reveals patterns of risk factors and enables early disease prediction, leading to significantly improved patient outcomes through timely diagnosis and reduced healthcare expenses. For example, DeepToxis able to predict the toxicity of chemicals, DeepChemis used to develop predictive models for drug discovery.
- Preventive: AI and ML enable personalised preventive strategies by analysing individual health data, identifying health risks and empowering proactive measures to prevent illnesses. For example, personalised preventive strategies, such as dietary and exercise plans, can be recommended to reduce the risk of developing cardiovascular, diabetes and other disease conditions.
- Participatory: AI and ML technologies facilitate patient engagement and involvement in their healthcare journey. Patients can actively

participate in decision-making processes and access health information more effectively, leading to improved overall healthcare outcomes. For example, patient-facing apps, virtual coaches, clinical decision support tools and many more.

- Personalised medicine: Personalised medicine is a branch of medicine, where AI and ML can be utilised to create tools that employ patient data, assisting healthcare professionals in making more precise and informed decisions regarding patient care. For example, IBM Watson is used for oncology, Google Health and many more.

To improve accuracy and predictability and reduce time investment, AI and ML are crucial in pharmaceutical Research and Development (R&D), aiding in designing drug molecules, screening them and predicting interactions. The general approaches applicable in the R&D of pharmaceutical products are shown in Figure 2.1.

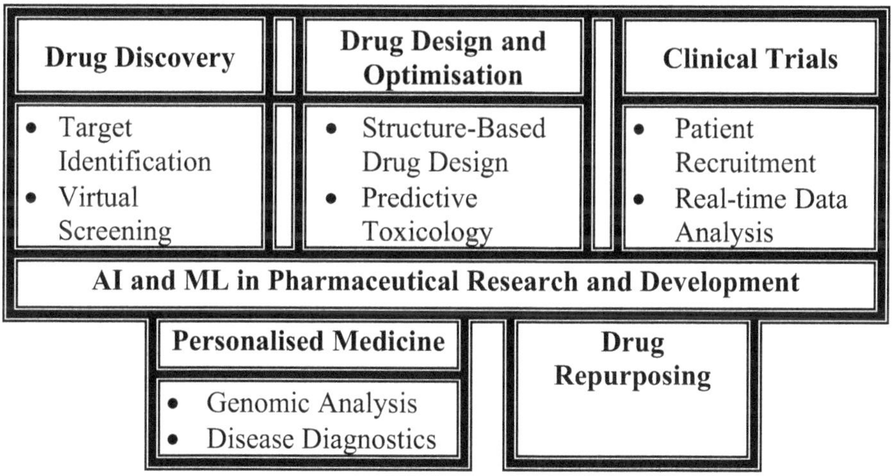

Figure 2.1 AI and ML in Pharmaceutical Research and Development.

2.2 AI and ML Derived Drug Discovery

Drug discovery is the systematic process of identifying and developing new medications to treat various diseases. The pharmaceutical industry aims to develop effective drugs faster, cheaper and better. AI and ML are rapidly transforming the drug discovery process. A number of AI and ML-driven drug compounds are currently in development, and some have already been approved for clinical use. Some AI and ML-derived drug compounds are shown in Table 2.1

Table 2.1 AI and ML Derived Drug Compounds.

Organisation / Company	Programme/ Compound	Treatment/ Description / Indication
Insilico Medicine	INS018_055	Idiopathic pulmonary fibrosis
	ISM3312	COVID-19
Exscientia	EXS74539	Neoplasms
	EXS73565	Haematology
BenevolentAI	BEN-2293	Atopic dermatitis
Structure Therapeutics	GSBR-1290	Type 2 diabetes Obesity
	ANPA-0073	Pulmonary arterial hypertension Idiopathic pulmonary fibrosis
Valo Health	OPL-0401	Diabetic retinopathy Diabetic complications
	OPL-0301	Post-myocardial infarction Acute kidney injury
Relay Therapeutics	RLY-2608	Solid tumors
Pharos iBio	PHI-101	Acute myeloid leukemia Ovarian cancer Radiation sensitiser Triple-negative breast cancer
Recursion	REC-2282	Cerebral cavernous malformation
	REC-228	Neurofibromatosis type 2
Evotec and Exscientia	EXS-21546	Solid tumors carrying high adenosine signatures

2.2.1 Drug Target Identification, Selection and Prioritisation with compound Screening and design

AI/ML technologies are currently playing a crucial role in early drug discovery, focusing on tasks such as drug target identification, selection, prioritisation, compound screening and drug design. In the early stages of drug development, identifying the most suitable biological targets for potential drug candidates is essential. AI and ML technologies are used to analyse scientific research, publications and large data sets collected from various sources. The increasing availability of complex data, including genomics, transcriptomics, proteomics and many more, from healthy individuals and those with specific diseases presents a valuable opportunity for choosing suitable drug targets. AI/ML models and algorithms aim to improve the process of identifying potential drug candidates virtually. AI and ML-derived drug discovery approaches are shown in Table 2.2.

Table 2.2 AI and ML-derived Drug Discovery Approaches.

Steps	Brief Description
Step 1 Identify the Problem	Problems identification is the initial phase of developing an AI and ML-based drug discovery model, which is crucial to ensure drug development as well as its success.
Step 2 Find, Prepare and Encode the Data	Finding, preparing and encoding data for AI and ML-based drug discovery models is a crucial step in the development of such models. The major factors include data collection and data preprocessing with feature encoding.
Step 3 Select Feature	The choice of feature selection strategies significantly affects the model's performance. In drug discovery, domain-specific features such as molecular descriptors (molecular weight, lipophilicity), biological activity measurements and structural properties are often critical.
Step 4 Split the data (Test/Training)	Splitting the data into training and testing processes helps to assess the model's performance on unseen data and detect potential overfitting.
Step 5 (Build the AI/ ML Model)	The development of AI and ML-based drug discovery models is an iterative process. The iterative process refers to the cyclic and repetitive nature of developing machine learning models and algorithms for various tasks related to drug discovery.
Step 6 Train the Model	Model training for drug discovery is also an iterative process that requires multiple cycles of experimentation and refinement. The trained model and relevant data must be saved for future use or deployment.
Step 7 Evaluate and Improve the Model	Evaluating and improving drug discovery models is an ongoing process that requires a combination of technical expertise, domain knowledge, and a commitment to continuous learning and refinement.
Step 8 Test the Model on Independent Data	Testing on independent data provides a valuable assessment of how well the model can generalise to real-world situations. Assessing its generalisation performance and ensuring it assists in making predictions on unseen data.

The databases offer a comprehensive view of around millions of compounds, establishing connections between their chemical makeup and biological, pharmacological and therapeutic characteristics. These often originate from diverse sources and are suitable for AI/ML techniques. Data from diverse sources (often in an unstructured format), is transformed into an organised rationale database. This data undergoes manual and automated entry and is subjected to rigorous quality parameters, as shown in Figure 2.2.

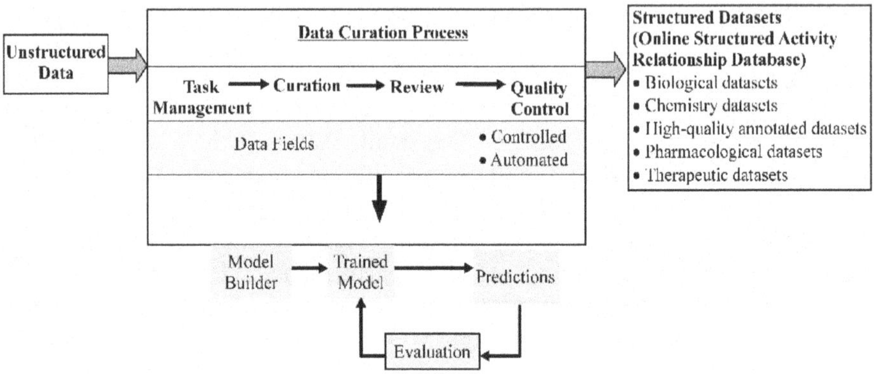

Figure 2.2 AI/ML for Drug Discovery.

The resulting structured datasets encompass information related to structure-activity relationships (SAR), physicochemical properties and ADMET (Absorption, Distribution, Metabolism, Excretion and Toxicity) parameters. These datasets are integrated into the platform to train AI and ML algorithms for creating models and predicting activity and properties, thereby aiding in identifying promising compounds and optimising lead candidates. High-quality annotated biological, chemistry, pharmacological and therapeutic datasets containing essential information for disease understanding, drug discovery and patient-related insights are structured for seamless integration into databases using standardised identifiers and controlled vocabularies. Some critical databases used in drug discovery for various purposes in AI and ML models are shown in Figure 2.3.

DeepChem	PubChem	DrugBank	COCONUT	ChEMBL	ChemDB
DGIdb	**Databases used in drug discovery for various purposes in AI and ML**				ZINC
LINCS (Library of Integrated Network-based Cellular Signatures)	CMap (Connectivity Map)	SIDER (Side Effect Resource)	Drug-Gene Interaction Database (DGIdb)	PDB (Protein Data Bank)	TTD (Therapeutic Target Database)

Figure 2.3 Databases used in drug discovery for various purposes in AI and ML.

The brief information related to the above databases is mentioned below:

- **ChEMBL:** A curated database of drug-like bioactive molecules bridging chemical, bioactivity and genomic data for drug discovery.
- **ChemDB:** An open database featuring small molecules and their fundamental physicochemical properties, accompanied by user-friendly cheminformatics tools for drug discovery.
- **CMap (Connectivity Map):** Generating and studying extensive perturbation datasets to enhance knowledge related to human diseases and expedite the discovery of new treatments.
- **COCONUT:** An open-source portal for natural products cheminformatics, natural product storage, search and analysis of natural products.
- **DeepChem:** A Python library for ML and Deep Learning with molecules and quantum data, making it easy to create, test and use models.
- **Drug Bank:** Free-access drug database for comprehensive drug information that is widely used for screening, design and metabolism prediction.
- **Drug-Gene Interaction Database (DGIdb):** A resource for identifying candidate genes and drugs within the druggable genome.
- **Library of Integrated Network-based Cellular Signatures (LINCS):** A database with gene data of millions of compounds, helping find new drug targets and predict drug effects.
- **Protein Data Bank (PDB):** Allowing scientific breakthroughs and education through access to experimentally determined 3D protein structures, computed structure models and the development of structural perspective on biology.
- **PubChem:** A public chemistry database with molecule details including structures, properties and biological activities.
- **Side Effect Resource (SIDER):** A database for drug side effects used in drug indication prediction, side effect analysis and identifying metabolic dysregulation.
- **Therapeutic Target Database (TTD):** A comprehensive database of referenced information on therapeutic protein and nucleic acid targets, associated diseases, pathways and corresponding drugs.
- **ZINC:** A freely accessible database comprising millions of commercially available compounds provided in readily dockable 3D formats designed for virtual screening.

Data curation is an activity that involves the systematic organization and management of data while ensuring quality. It is important to ensure data consistency through access and usability throughout the lifecycle. Data corruption, loss and misinterpretation are some of the risks to ensure that the data is useful to the researchers. Data curation is an essential step in the drug discovery process. It promotes the development of new, better and more effective drugs by assisting researchers in identifying new drug targets, designing and testing new drugs and predicting drug success rates in clinical trials. These drug discovery activities use several strategies to improve data curation efficiency and effectiveness.

The data curation software is the backbone of drug discovery by enabling efficient pooling, organization and analysis of data from different types and sources. Some example data curation software are mentioned below:

- OmicsOffice and RedCap: These are used for data quality assurance, ensuring the data collected is accurate and reliable.
- BioPortal and SADI: These tools are essential for semantic integration, which helps in meaningful data aggregation.
- LabKey Server and Benchling: These platforms support collaboration and knowledge sharing between research teams.
- BIOVIA Pipeline Pilot and TIBCO Spotfire: The tools having data integration capabilities allow data from different sources to be easily combined.

Cloud Computing: Cloud computing is transforming drug discovery by offering on-demand resources. Cloud computing allows researchers to analyse vast amounts of data, collaborate globally and hold AI/ML for tasks like virtual screening, all at a lower cost. Examples include storing cancer patient data in "*The Cancer Genome Atlas (TCGA)*" cloud and using cloud-based platforms to design new drugs and manage clinical trials.

ML algorithms have significantly advanced drug discovery that benefits pharmaceutical companies. They are used to predict chemical, biological and physical characteristics of compounds, find new drug uses, predict drug-protein interactions and optimise molecule bioactivity.

2.3 Random Forest (RF) and Naive Bayesian (NB) in Pharmaceutical Research and Development

Random forest is an impactful machine learning technique, which combines the predictions of multiple decision trees to make an accurate prediction. This technique is an intelligent decision making system for finding pattern in data and in drug discovery process. The RF is being utilized in drug discovery process is different ways like,

- *Prediction of drug activity:* The data of different molecules with known activities for a given target is utilized to develop a model by RF. This model can easily predict the effectiveness of new drug candidate.
- *Identify new drug targets:* The potential drug targets can be identified by comparing the gene expression levels in healthy and diseased tissues.
- *Domain improvement in drug design:* The properties like binding affinity for target protein, which can indicate potential toxicity can be predicted by RF and thereby enhancing the drug design process.

2.3.1 Naive Bayesian (NB)

NB is a machine learning algorithm having many applications specifically in drug discovery. It can be used for a small size of datasets and relatively simple to train and interpret. The model developed by NB is used to predict potential drug targets in drug discovery process. The NB model integrates large amount of data from multiple sources including the gene expression data and data with known side effects resulting in higher accuracy. This approach is also used for drug target prediction and for protein-drug interactions. The different datasets are combined to improve the accuracy of the prediction by Bayesian Machine Learning (BML) approach. The examples includes,

- ***Chemical structure data:*** The accurate information about the chemical structure or the content of drug molecules is accurately provided.
- ***Binding affinity data:*** It indicates the binding of drug molecules with different proteins.
- ***Gene expression data:*** It represents the gene expression in cells and tissues.
- ***Proteomics data:*** The data represents the proteins forms in biological samples.

The diverse set of data is utilized for prediction of proteins as therapeutic target by BML algorithms. For example, the BANDIT platform includes the drug target prediction tools. The Bayesian approach is utilized for investigation of several forms of data in combined form using BANDIT. The data from multiple sources is merged to provide the predictions.

2.3.2 Support Vector Machines (SVMs)

SVMs have dominated various applications for drug discovery. SVM classifies compounds as possible medications based on past data. Scientists collect the data on molecular attributes, train SVMs to discriminate known medicines from non-drugs accurately and then use them to forecast novel compounds as medications. One area that clearly indicates excellent potential for SVM in managing large, complex and high-dimensional data is bioinformatics, which is used to identify promising drug candidates. For example, training an SVM to analyze the properties of a compound with the sequence or structure of a protein can yield a suitable model. This combined analysis helps identify promising new drug candidates, particularly for poorly understood targets (orphan targets).

2.4 Virtual Screening (VS)

VS is a critical tool in drug development that leverages ML as a subset of AI to efficiently search vast compound databases, enhancing the identification of potential drug leads. AL/ML for VS entails the creation of a filtered training dataset containing known active and inactive compounds. Following model training and validation, it is deployed on novel databases to screen for compounds with desired drug target binding activity as shown in Figure 2.4. The initial step in VS involves assembling a compound database, often sourced from publicly available chemogenomics libraries like ChEMBL, PubChem, ZINC and many more. Each contains millions of compounds with structural and target information. Pharmaceutical companies also access in-house databases, including compounds from potentially unsuccessful clinical trials. Regardless of the source, the dataset undergoes further filtering to eliminate nonviable compounds and reduce false positives. Once the dataset is prepared, screening can be performed through

- Ligand-based virtual screening (LBVS)
- Structure-based virtual screening (SBVS), or
- Combination of both

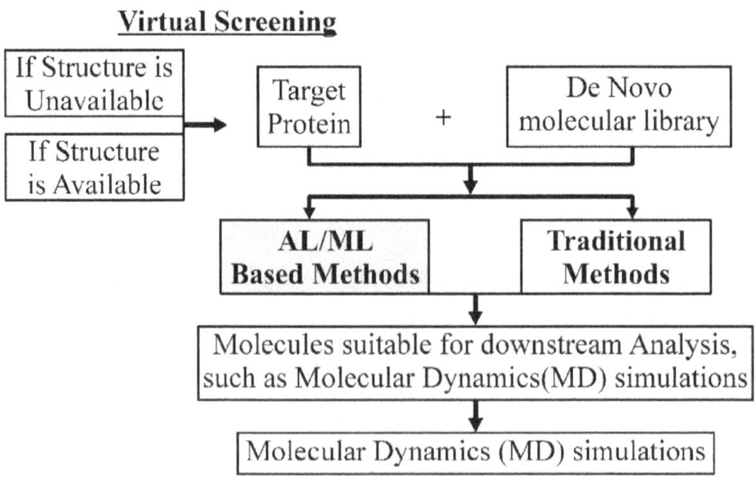

Figure 2.4 Virtual Screening with modern AI/ML methods.

Structure-based virtual screening primarily assesses ligand and target binding site structures to evaluate the likelihood of binding using docking techniques. This method depends on knowledge of the compound and target structures. In contrast, LBVS relies on known active substances and molecular and chemical properties of the test compounds and do not require structural data. LBVS works on the basis that undiscovered active substances will share some chemical characteristics with known ones. Examples of AI and ML-based tools for virtual screening are:

- **ZairaChem:** An automated AI/ML pipeline tailored for quick and straightforward deployment in resource-constrained environments, facilitating QSAR/QSPR modeling.
- **AlphaFold:** An AI system developed by DeepMind, proficient in predicting the three-dimensional structure of proteins from their amino acid sequences, consistently delivering accuracy comparable to the experimental results.

The AI/ML models trained on well-validated data can analyse larger datasets better to understand the potential structure and function of targets, allowing more accurate investigation and prediction of their roles in disease pathways. While AI and ML significantly improve target identification and prioritization, more research is needed to determine whether drug targets identified by AI and ML are involved in disease.

Predicting drug toxicity is essential to drug development and pharmacology in general. Before a drug is approved for clinical use, it is tested for potential toxicity in an organism. This highly complex, multifaceted task requires a wide range of technologies and data sources.

2.5 Prediction of Safety, Efficacy and Toxicity (SET)

In recent years, there has been growing interest in using AI and ML to predict drug predictive safety, efficacy and toxicity. AI predicts the outcomes of drug candidates based on their chemical structure, *in vitro/in vivo* biological activity and clinical trial results. AI and ML models, after training on previous data, find patterns and predict new drug predictive safety, efficacy and toxicity to assist researchers at various decision-making stages. AI and ML models are trained on comprehensive datasets containing toxic and non-toxic compounds to obtain patterns associated with predictive safety, efficacy and toxicity. Once trained, these models allow for predicting various parameters, including predictive safety, efficacy and toxicity and others in drug compounds, without requiring costly and time-consuming testing, as shown in Figure 2.5.

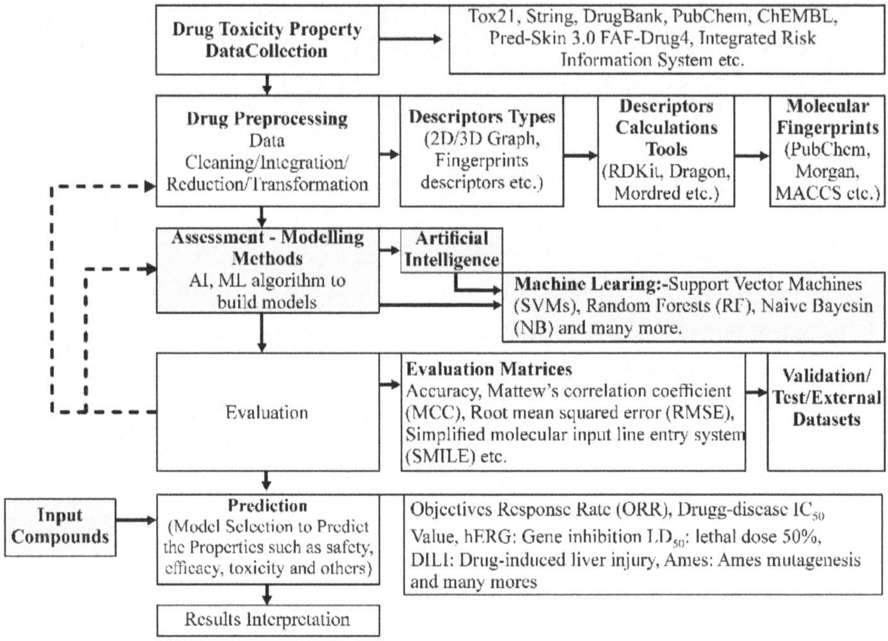

Figure 2.5 Process flow for Safety, Efficacy and Toxicity (SET) prediction models.

For predicting Safety, Efficacy and Toxicity (SET) using AI and ML models, access to large and diverse datasets of chemical compounds and their associated Safety, Efficacy and Toxicity (SET) details are required. Several sources of public data are valuable for training and validating AI-based drug Safety, Efficacy and Toxicity (SET) prediction models. Some critical public data sources for Safety, Efficacy and Toxicity (SET) prediction are shown in Figure 2.6.

SIDER	Tox21	CompTox	UniProt	HelixADMET
Schrodinger Maestro	LiverTox	**AI and ML based Safety, Efficacy and Toxicity Prediction Databases**	DSSTox	XenoSit
Small Molecule Pathway Database (SMPD)	Genetic Toxicology Data Bank (GENE-TOX)	Drug-Induced Liver Injury Rank (DILIrank)	Gene Expression Omnibus (GEO)	FAF-Drug4

Figure 2.6 AI and ML based Safety, Efficacy and Toxicity Prediction Databases.

The advantages of AI and ML-based Safety, Efficacy and Toxicity (SET) prediction models include:

- **Accuracy:** These models have proved much better accuracy in predicting compound Safety, Efficacy and Toxicity (SET) in comparison to traditional methods.
- **Cost-Effectiveness:** AI models are more affordable as compared to conventional methods. Their low development and utilisation costs result in significant cost reductions.
- **Speed and efficiency:** The developed AI/ML models can produce faster results with instant assessments of a compound's Safety, Efficacy and Toxicity (SET). The traditional testing methods may take weeks or even months to deliver results. The quickness and effectiveness of AI models significantly improve productivity and decision-making.
- **Ethical Considerations:** Researchers or organisations may eliminate animal experimentation by using AI to forecast Safety, Efficacy and Toxicity (SET), which addresses and aligns with moral issues. This strategy allows them to follow contemporary ethical norms by endorsing cruelty-free testing procedures.

Digital technology immensely impacted pharmaceutical research and development, causing significant changes in industry processes and capabilities. Integrating digital-based tools like AI, ML and other digital technologies has increased the rate of drug discovery and development. AI and ML have become very powerful tools in pharmaceutical research and development. Advanced technologies promote significant advances in efficiency, precision and safety in research and development. AI and ML evolved inseparably to become part of pharmaceutical research and development tools, changing the industrial approach towards drug development and healthcare. Their application is bound to make a difference in creating novel treatments and improving patient outcomes for the betterment of society.

Proposed Questions

Long Answer Type Questions (10 Marks Each)

1. Describe Safety, Efficacy and Toxicity (SET) predictions using AI/ML and their importance in pharmaceutical research and development.
2. Describe the feature engineering process in the context of SVMs for drug discovery with suitable examples.

3. Describe the approaches of virtual screening, highlighting their strengths and limitations.
4. Discuss the key features of Random Forest in drug discovery.

Short Answer Type Questions (5 Marks Each)

1. Discuss the potential impact of personalised medicine facilitated by AI and ML technologies.
2. What role do AI and ML techniques play in drug compound development?
3. Discuss the role of Artificial Intelligence (AI) and Machine Learning (ML) in revolutionising drug discovery and personalised medicine.
4. Evaluate the significance of the 4Ps approaches in assessing drug efficacy and safety through AI and ML techniques.
5. Identify and explain specific tools or methodologies employed in AI and ML-driven drug discovery processes.

Very Short Questions (1 Mark)

1. What is the primary role of AI and ML in pharmaceutical research and development?
2. Define the process of drug target identification in the context of AI and ML.
3. How do machine learning algorithms assist in compound screening and design?
4. Name one commonly used AI/ML enabled database in drug discovery.
5. Give an example of a predictive modeling algorithm used for drug discovery.
6. What is virtual screening and how does it contribute to drug discovery?
7. Explain the significance of predictive safety, efficacy and toxicity modeling in pharmaceutical sciences.
8. Name one machine learning technique often employed in drug discovery for its predictive capabilities.
9. Describe the importance of data curation in AI and ML applications for pharmaceutical research.
10. Discuss the transformative potential of AI and ML in pharmaceutical sciences.

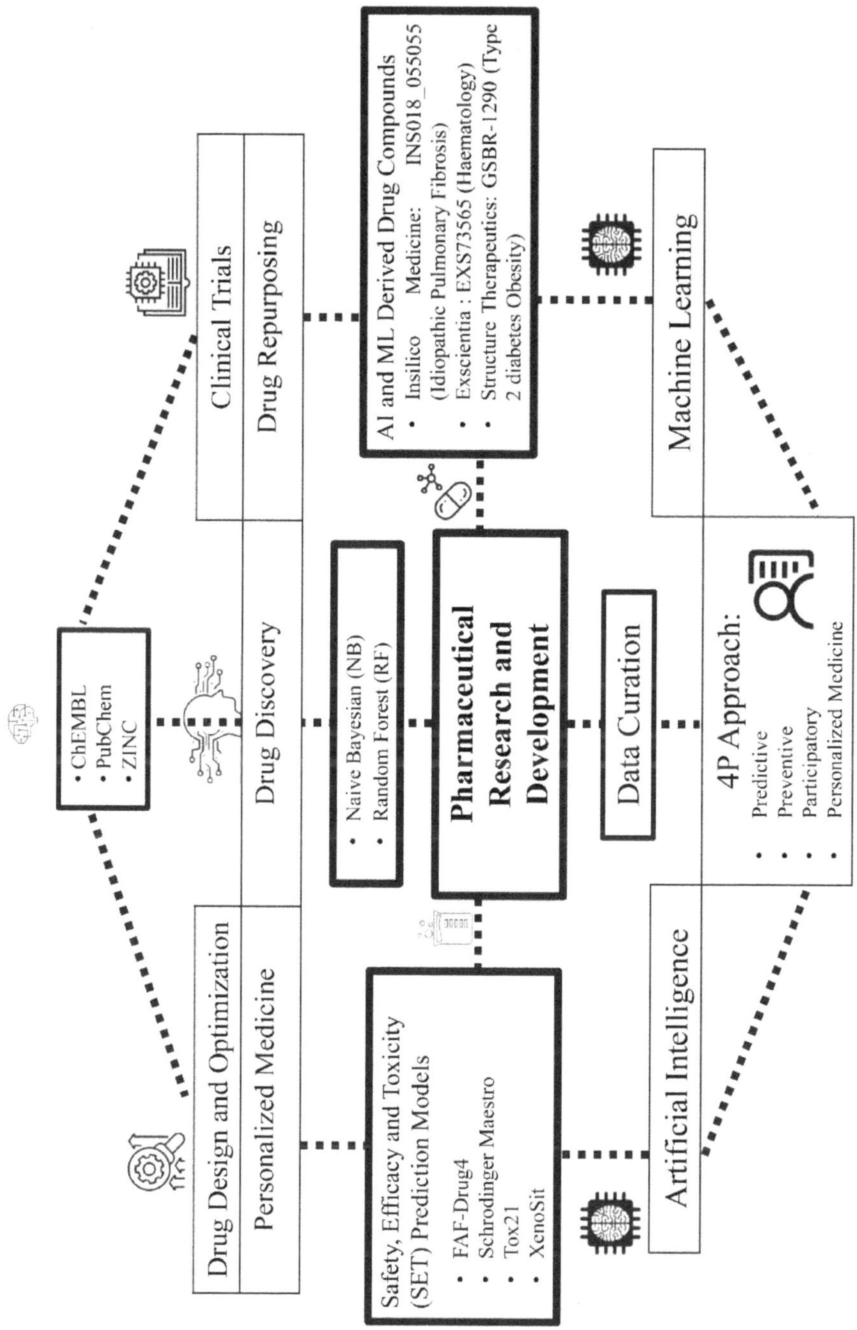

Drug Design and Optimization
Personalized Medicine
ChEMBL
PubChem
ZINC
Drug Discovery
Clinical Trials
Drug Repurposing
Safety, Efficacy and Toxicity (SET) Prediction Models
FAF-Drug4
Schrodinger Maestro
Tox21
XenoSit
Naive Bayesian (NB)
Random Forest (RF)
Pharmaceutical Research and Development
AI and ML Derived Drug Compounds
Insilico Medicine: INS018_055055 (Idiopathic Pulmonary Fibrosis)
Exscientia : EXS73565 (Haematology)
Structure Therapeutics: GSBR-1290 (Type 2 diabetes Obesity)
Data Curation
Artificial Intelligence
Machine Learning
4P Approach:
Predictive
Preventive
Participatory
Personalized Medicine

CHAPTER 3

AI and ML in the Modern Pharmaceutical Sector

3.1 Introduction

The pharmaceutical sector has rapidly changed over the past few years due to the seamless merging of Artificial Intelligence (AI) and Machine Learning (ML). These changes are bringing rapid advancements in pharmaceutical products and services at any stage, be it in development or management. Innovation and research-driven approach are two words that characterise the modern pharmaceutical sector. Drugs and devices are discovered, developed, manufactured and distributed to improve human health. There is constant change over time with new technologies and discoveries.

Innovation, collaboration and patient-centricity are the keys to the success of the modern pharmaceutical sector. Technological advancements, changes in the regulatory environment, demographic changes and consumer expectations drive significant revisions. More precisely, it means that the digitalisation of data has advanced to a stage where it has become possible to collect, test and use vast knowledge to solve challenges at all levels of pharmaceutical products and services. Digitisation allows AI and ML to be used to process large amounts of data through automation.

On the other hand, advancements in biotechnology are leading to radical changes in drug development and manufacturing processes. Some of these techniques, including genetic engineering and monoclonal antibody therapies, lead to more focused therapies. This is due to the significant emphasis on personalised medicine, with individualised treatment based on genetic factors and lifestyle. This leads to more accurate and effective treatments with fewer side effects.

The integration of digital technologies such as telemedicine and wearable devices is revolutionising healthcare delivery and patient management. This change allows remote monitoring, real-time data collection, personalised intervention and many more. Additionally, pharmaceutical companies are attempting to demonstrate the affordability and accessibility of their products and services, in view of pricing transparency and regulatory changes. These companies increasingly collaborate with academic institutions, research organisations and technology firms to promote innovation. These partnerships encourage the exchange of knowledge and access to new technologies. The focus is on developing treatments for rare diseases, with incentives and thereby encouraging Research and Development (R&D) in this area. In addition, companies are focusing on implementing sustainable practices in manufacturing, packaging and distribution processes.

Some of the cutting-edge technologies in the current pharmaceutical sector by integrity the AI and ML are as shown in Figure 3.1.

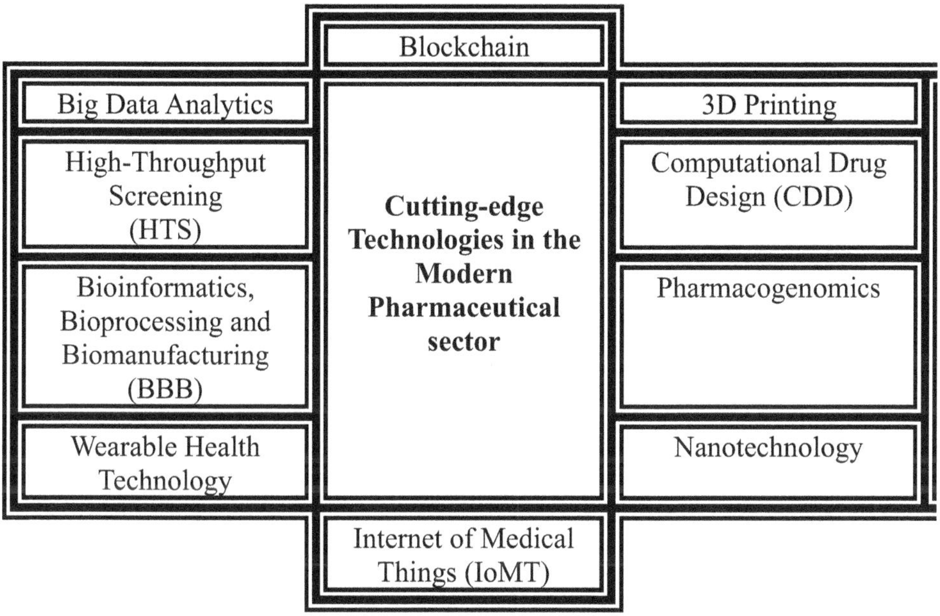

Figure 3.1 Cutting-edge Technologies in the Modern Pharmaceutical Sector.

Advanced tools and technologies are used in the modern pharmaceutical sector to improve product discovery, development, distribution, etc. High-Throughput Screening (HTS) automates the screening of many chemical compounds to identify potential drug candidates efficiently. Computational Drug Design (CDD) predicts how drugs interact with their target molecules and optimises their properties for better efficacy and safety. Bioinformatics analyses biological data to identify promising drug targets and gain insights into disease mechanisms. Pharmacogenomics investigates how genetic variations influence individual medication responses, aiding in personalised treatment approaches. Big data analytics studies analyse large amounts of data to determine drug safety, efficacy and market trends. It guides decisions at each stage of the process. Bioprocessing technologies involving cell culture, fermentation and purification are used to manufacture biopharmaceuticals. Nanotechnology creates nano drug delivery systems to make treatments more concentrated and effective. 3D printing technology precisely manufactures individual drugs as well as dosage forms. Blockchain technology maintains the security and efficiency of the pharmaceutical supply chain. It provides traceability, which helps to ensure compliance with medication regulations. The Internet of Medical Things (IoMT) is a network of sensors and interconnected medical devices that play a crucial role in the modern healthcare sector. These IoMT devices remotely monitor the patient's vital signs, activity levels, medication adherence and other health-related parameters. By continuously collecting current and relevant health data, IoMT allows healthcare experts to track patients remotely for appropriate intervention at the right time for personalised care. These IoMT devices enable the patient to adhere more to the medication schedule by providing reminders regarding taking medications on time. Wearable Health Technology (WHT) refers to devices that patients wear to track health parameters and medication adherence, hence both remote healthcare delivery and clinical trials with continuous real-time data. IoMT and WHT have been integrated to achieve better patient outcomes, increase access to health care and advance medical research. AI and ML enable pharmaceutical research & development is providing drugs more quickly and efficiently. Driving innovation & progress in the industry for better patient outcomes and healthcare delivery.

3.2 Importance of AI and ML in Pharmaceuticals

The pharmaceutical sector uses AI and ML very efficiently on a wide scale. The growing population stands to benefit from AI and ML deployment in the pharmaceutical industry. Individualised medication management and round-the-clock support are offered to patients, enhancing healthcare support and access. Healthcare costs may be minimised by AI and ML, which reduces errors and prevent harmful interactions. The workload of healthcare professionals may be lightened by AI and ML, which constantly enable them to focus on critical tasks. Integrating AI and ML into the pharmaceutical sector enhances medical outcomes, lowers expenses, increases access to medical services and improves Quality of Life (QoL). AI and ML in the pharmaceutical industry also improve the QoL by enhancing treatment efficacy, reducing side effects, providing faster access to therapies, managing chronic diseases, offering patient support, improving healthcare access, enhancing emotional well-being and many more. The pharmaceutical sector is presently utilising both conventional and modern methods. The difference between conventional and modern methods is shown in Table 3.1. The integration of AI and ML technologies has significantly impacted the modern pharmaceutical sector. New technologies are emerging in the pharmaceutical industry and are carefully adopted.

Table 3.1 Applications of Conventional Methods and Modern Methods in Pharmaceutical Sciences.

Applications	Conventional Methods	Modern Methods
Drug Discovery	Manual screening of compounds	Virtual screening, molecular docking, QSAR models and many more.
Drug Repurposing	Laborious experimentation and literature review	AI /ML algorithms analysing large datasets for potential matches
Clinical Trials Optimisation	Slow recruitment and data analysis	AI /ML-powered patient recruitment and predictive analytics
Personalised Medicine	Broad treatment protocols	AI/ML motivated patient data analysis for tailored treatments
Pharmacovigilance	Manual adverse event reporting and analysis	Automated adverse event detection and signal detection
Drug Formulation Design	Trial and error experiments, Quality by Design (QbD)	AI/ML-driven formulation prediction and optimisation
Precision Medicine	Limited genomic analysis	AI/ ML-associated genomic analysis for precise treatment plans
Regulatory Compliance	Manual review of documents and compliance checks	AI/ ML-based regulatory compliance automation (Regulatory Information Management System)
Drug Safety Assessment	Manual evaluation of safety data	AI /ML algorithms for real-time safety monitoring and analysis
Supply Chain Optimisation	Manual forecasting and inventory management	AI /ML-driven demand forecasting and supply chain optimisation

3.3 Role of Pharmacist in the Modern Pharmaceutical Sector

Integrating AI and ML technologies empowers pharmacists to enhance patient care, improve medication safety, and drive innovation in the pharmaceutical sector, eventually optimising medication therapy outcomes and advancing healthcare delivery. Pharmacists play a crucial role in the modern pharmaceutical sector, which is evolving with the integration of AI and ML technologies. Modern technologies are utilised in various aspects of pharmacy practice, including drug discovery, personalised medicine, medication therapy management, etc. Figure 3.2 highlights the role of pharmacist/chemists in the modern pharmaceutical sector.

Drug Discovery and Development	**Role of Pharmacists in the Modern Pharmaceutical Sector**	Personalised Medicine
Drug Interaction and Adverse Event Monitoring		Clinical Decision Support Systems
Medication Therapy Management (MTM)		Supply Chain Management
Patient Education and Counseling		Quality Assurance and Regulatory Compliance
Telepharmacy Services		Collaborative Care

Figure 3.2 Role of Pharmacists in the Modern Pharmaceutical Sector.

The patient data is analyzed by the pharmacist in order to improve medical outcomes by personalized medications and provide counselling and interventions to identify medication related issues. The patient safety and optimized healthcare outcomes are ensured by the pharmacist in modern pharmaceutical sector. In addition, with the help of data analytics, the pharmacist validate the findings of AI and ML algorithms in drug discovery and development process and also ensure the efficacy and safety of drug candidates.

The AI and ML tools are enabling the pharmacist to reduce risk of medications by tracking real-time interventions and other adverse drug events. The collaboration between the computer professionals (software developers) and pharmacist is helping in developing a robust clinical decision-support system following the applicable regulations. The optimization of inventory management, predicting the demands, preventing the shortage and efficient availability of medication is feasible by the use of AI/ML tools by the pharmacist. These AI/ML tools can easily provide the patient education and counselling and empowering the patients to make health care decisions. The pharmacist also makes sure that the medications should meet the safety standards as per regulatory guidelines and thereby contribute in quality assurance and compliance efforts. The remote communities are provided with telepharmacy services and patient is provided with best possible drug therapy by health care providers to have the utmost care.

The modern pharmaceutical industry equipped with AI/ML technology is providing breakthrough in designing, manufacturing and marketing of variety of products and services related to human health. These new technologies and discoveries are providing the innovative treatment options for the patients.

3.4 AI/ML Based Medical Devices (MDs)

In today's world, the medical devices are essential part of healthcare, wellness and Quality of Life (QoL). The various applications of Medical Devices (MDs) include the monitoring, management and treatment across a wider range of disease conditions. The MDs integrated with digital technologies are transforming health and wellness up to a large extent and becoming much more important in healthcare. The simple objects like tongue depression and sophisticated system like robotic surgical instruments are examples of these MDs. The diverse MDs are used for the purpose of diagnosis, prevention and treatment of disease by healthcare professionals.

The tasks like surgery are also feasible by means of MDs. An individual or a patient can easily make the decision regarding the life style and health using the activity trackers and wearable devices such as smart watches. These wearable devices can continuously monitor health and metrics. These wearable devices are the lifeline in treating the chronic medical disorder when connected to different medical devices or tools such as insulin pumps or continuous glucose monitors. The combinations of smart devices with medical devices are improving the QoL by means of constant monitoring and timely interventions.

The telemonitoring, diagnosis for early detection of disease and treatment options for the conditions like pain/mobility and tools for people with disabilities are also supported by medical devices. The contribution of MDs also includes the wellness monitoring, safety, innovation, health care access and advanced telemedicine. These medical devices have intended use and some level of risk.

The MDs are regulated for safety and efficacy as well. The designing, manufacturing and distribution of the medical devices are ensured by regulatory agencies to meet the highest standard of patient safety. The quality and safety of these medical devices is essential for market approval and should be in compliance with the regulatory guidelines. The treatment outcomes and patient care have been improved by use of these MDs like X-ray machine, pacemakers, etc.

The medical devices, which does not require any physical hardware are represented as Software as Medical Devices (SaMD). The SaMD assist in diagnosis, treatment and monitoring human disease. Unlike other medical devices, its computer platforms differ. Examples include health apps that diagnose diseases, software to read images from medical scanning devices and algorithms to analyse patient data. Undoubtedly, SaMD plays an essential role in modern healthcare by developing innovative solutions to healthcare problems. Regulatory agencies classify SaMD according to the level of risk. Their purpose is to guide manufacturers towards achieving safety, effectiveness and quality. The dynamic nature of SaMD requires periodic changes in its development, validation and approval. With each new digital technological advancement, SaMD will become integral to healthcare as a treatment option in digital therapeutics (DTx), providing quality care and improving patient outcomes. AI and ML are transforming the medical device industry, providing innovative solutions across a wide range of healthcare domains, as shown in Table 3.2. Table 3.3 and also highlights the comparison of Medical Devices (MDs) and Software as Medical Devices (SAMD).

Table 3.2 Applications of AI/ML-Based Medical Devices (MDs).

Medical Devices	Brief Information
Diagnostic Imaging	AI/ML is integrated into magnetic resonance imaging (MRI), computed tomography (CT) scans and X-rays to provide accurate diagnosis and disease progression prediction.
Healthcare Chatbots	Virtual assistants provide health advice, answer queries and schedule appointments using Natural Language Processing (NLP).
Mental Health Monitoring	AI/ML analyses speech and facial expressions to detect mental health disorders and assist in intervention.
Personalised Medicine	AI analyses genetic, clinical and lifestyle data for tailored treatment plans and improve outcomes.
Predictive Analytics	Analyses Electronic Health Records (EHRs) and healthcare data to predict patient outcomes, aiding decision-making.
Remote Patient Monitoring	Allows continuous monitoring outside healthcare settings, detecting deviations for early intervention.
Robot-Assisted Surgery	Surgical robots with AI/ML assist surgeons with precise procedures, analysing data in real-time.
Smart Prosthetics and Orthotics	AI/ML-controlled devices adapt to user preferences and improve functionality over time.
Wearable Health Monitors	In real-time, devices monitor vital signs like heart rate, blood pressure and glucose levels.

Table 3.3 Comparison between Medical Devices (MDs) and Software as Medical Devices (SaMD).

Medical Devices	Software as Medical Devices (SaMD)
Physical apparatus or instruments	Software intended for medical purposes without hardware
Regulatory authorities Clearance, Conformité Européenne (CE) mark and other regulatory agencies	Specific regulatory frameworks for software
Hardware engineering, extensive testing	Software engineering, algorithm development and validation
Longer lifecycles and physical components	Shorter lifecycles due to rapid software advancements or updates
Physical harm due to malfunction or misuse	Data security, software bugs, incorrect algorithm outputs
Physical installation and periodic servicing	Software installation and remote updates
Clinical trials and performance testing	Algorithm validation and software testing
Mainly the buttons, displays and physical controls	Graphical user interface, touch screens and digital controls
Material safety and biocompatibility	Data security, encryption and protection against cyber threats
Wired or wireless connections	Internet connectivity, cloud services, interoperability
Training for operation and maintenance	User training for software use, updates and troubleshooting
Disposal of physical components and waste management	Energy consumption, carbon footprint and electronic waste

Advanced algorithms have enabled AI/ML-powered medical tools to change the face of healthcare in the 21st century. They increase accuracy, efficiency and personal care. The aim is to transform healthcare delivery and patient monitoring, empowering providers to benefit the patients globally. Table 3.4 shows the AI/ML-enabled medical devices approved/cleared by the different regulatory authorities.

Table 3.4 AI/ML-Enabled Medical Devices.

Device Name	Purpose	Company Name
Irregular Rhythm Notification Feature (IRNF)	Cardiovascular	Apple Inc.
EyeArt v2.2.0	Ophthalmic	Eyenuk, Inc
AI-Rad Companion (Cardiovascular)	Radiology	Siemens Medical Solutions
Belun Sleep System BLS-10	Anesthesiology	Belun Technology Company Limited
BrainInsight	Radiology	Hyperfine Inc.
Skout Software	Gastroenterology/Urology	Iterative Scopes Inc.
DeepRhythmAI	Cardiovascular	Medicalgorithmics S.A.
Atrial Fibrillation History Feature	Cardiovascular	Apple Inc.
OnQ Neuro	Radiology	CorTechs Labs Inc.
BriefCase	Radiology	Aidoc Medical Ltd.
WellDoc BlueStar	General Hospital	WellDoc Inc.
Sight OLO	Hematology	Sight Diagnostics Ltd.
ACR | LAB Urine Analysis Test System	Clinical Chemistry	Healthy.Io Ltd.
Sozo	Gastroenterology-Urology	ImpediMed Ltd.
Wave Clinical Platform	Cardiovascular	Excel Medical Electronics, LLC
MATRx Plus	Anesthesiology	Zephyr Sleep Technologies
Tyto Stethoscope	Cardiovascular	Tyto Care Ltd.
Dario Blood Glucose Monitoring System	Clinical Chemistry	LabStyle Innovations Ltd.
SnoreSounds	Anesthesiology	Appian Medical Inc.
MALDI Biotyper CA (MBT-CA) System	Microbiology	Bruker Daltonics Inc.
CellaVision DM96 Automatic Hematology Analyzer	Hematology	Cella Vision AB

3.4.1 Digital Therapeutics (DTx)

Digital therapeutics (DTx) are an emerging form of pharmaceutical product as medical devices that use digital technologies such as mobile apps and software programs to provide evidence-based interventions for the prevention, management or treatment of a medical condition. These interventions are designed and packaged to change behaviour and improve clinical health outcomes. They are typically implemented using techniques based on behavioural psychology, cognitive behavioural therapy, mindfulness and other evidence-based practices. Regulatory bodies are accepting DTx as a separate class of medical products. Some DTx have been cleared or approved as medical devices, focusing on clinical data to demonstrate their safety and efficacy.

DTx products include reSET for Attention Deficit Hyperactivity Disorder (ADHD), EndeavorRx for attention deficit hyperactivity disorder, Somryst for sleep disorders (digitally tracked as well as analyse behaviour) and Vremo for chronic pain therapy. Waylens for managing attention deficit hyperactivity disorder via the smartphone app.

AI/ML integration into DTx has the potential to improve performance and personalisation significantly. AI algorithms can analyse user data, allowing developers to provide adaptive interventions, predictions on health outcomes, insights into user behaviour, real-time feedback & coaching and the ability to improve interventions continually. DTx in healthcare is a new frontier with opportunities to bring innovative solutions for better health outcomes in providing care. When DTx is combined with AI/ML, such integration amplifies the benefits, resulting in a personalised, adaptive and data-driven intervention that genuinely changes the course of healthcare delivery and empowers healthcare professionals with decentralised solutions. It also empowers the digital treatment of patients.

3.5 AI/ML for Medical Imaging and Analysis

The accurate, timely diagnosis and prognosis are essential in healthcare profession. AI and ML play crucial roles in medical imaging and analysis by enabling the construction of models for disease detection and providing tools for diagnosis, prognosis and risk assessment to aid medical decision-making. Medical imaging has become increasingly utilised due to the development of back-propagation Deep-Learning AI systems, which are claimed to offer reliable diagnosis. Database systems capable of computerised medical image scanning and big data configuration have emerged as automated analytical systems. AI/ ML applied to medical imaging facilitate automated illness diagnosis, histology, stage or subtype characterisation and patient classification based on response to therapy or prognosis. AI-powered analytical techniques can expedite the diagnostic process and enhance diagnostic precision. AI/ML has numerous critical applications in Medical Image Analysis (MIA), starting from image acquisition, which utilises medical imaging modalities to capture anatomical or functional data and involves various typical operations. Key uses of AI/ML in medical imaging and analysis include:

- **Disease detection and diagnosis:** Patterns in medical images indicative of disease can be identified by AI algorithms, aiding in earlier and more accurate disease detection, such as spotting tumors in mammograms or signs of Alzheimer's disease in brain scans.
- **Risk assessment:** AI/ML models are able to evaluate a patient's risk of developing a specific disease based on their medical images and other health data, leading to personalised prevention plans.
- **Treatment planning:** AI/ML can assist healthcare professionals in planning disease treatments, like segmenting tumors in images to guide radiation therapy.
- **Workflow improvement:** AI automation can handle time-consuming tasks in medical image analysis, freeing up radiologists' time for more complex analysis.

Although the use of AI/ML in medical imaging is still emerging, it holds the potential to transform disease diagnosis and treatment. Some examples are:

- Brainomix 360 is a FDA-approved software which utilises advanced AI algorithms to aid clinicians in the real-time interpretation of brain scans for stroke patients, facilitating appropriate treatment delivery.
- syngo.CT Lung CAD (Computer Aided Detection) is an automated second reader tool designed to aid radiologists in detecting solid pulmonary nodules in chest CT examinations. It operates as an adjunctive tool, alerting radiologists to potentially overlooked regions of interest.
- Sonio products (detect and pro) have recently received FDA endorsement for its software. The Sonio detect software, a cutting-edge AI helper, enhances the accuracy and effectiveness of ultrasound examinations, promising to revolutionise fetal examination.

There are several more examples of AI/ ML-based medical imaging analysis such as ANDI, UltraSight AI Guidance, OptimMRI, Omnispace, ECHELON Synergy MRI system, Spine CAMP™, Axial3D Insight and HepaFatSmart (V2.0.0) and many more. AI and ML are transforming the field of medical imaging and analysis. Through the application of these powerful techniques to medical images like X-rays, CT scans and MRIs, new insights into diseases can be gained, diagnoses can be improved and better patient care can be provided.

3.6 AI and ML for Predictive Maintenance and Remote Monitoring

Predictive maintenance and remote monitoring are experiencing a significant evolution due to AI and ML. These pharmaceutical and healthcare industry advancements are critical to ensure equipment reliability and patient safety. The Internet of Things (IoT) is at the centre of these advancements, which serve as the foundation for predictive maintenance, driving the business forward in different areas:

- **IoT sensor for data collection:** Pharmaceutical and healthcare facilities uses a variety of sensors installed in or attached to machines in vulnerable locations to collect device data. These sensors can continuously monitor critical parameters such as vibration, temperature, pressure and energy consumption. These are used to monitor medical equipment and pharmaceutical production operations to obtain the optimal conditions.
- **Data transmission for centralised analysis:** Wireless data transmission from sensors to a cloud platform or local server enables easy access to device data across the facility and a centralised approach for study. This information allows HCPs (Health Care Professionals) to monitor the health of patients and pharmaceutical specialists to closely monitor the health of the equipment and make informed decisions about maintenance and operation.
- **Role of IoT in Predictive Maintenance:** Pharmaceutical and healthcare industries are benefitted from the real-time data stream of IoT disseminated through AI/ML algorithms. This monitoring enables early detection of potential problems by capturing subtle changes in sensor data. For example, in the healthcare manufacturing industry, IoT helps to detect anomalies in the performance of the MDs or any other equipment, allowing timely intervention to prevent disruptions in patient care.

AI /ML are the brains behind remote monitoring systems in all healthcare facilities. These technologies analyse historical data to establish normal equipment behaviour, detect anomalies and accurately estimate failure probabilities. Such a proactive strategy enables automated alerts to healthcare professionals for early intervention and timely action and enhances decision-making regarding scheduling maintenance and resource planning. For example, in the case of remote patient monitoring, wearable sensors collect health data from patients who are at risk of developing various chronic conditions. The same information is streamed to AI/ML in real time to analyse anomalies in vital signs that could mean deterioration in the patient's condition. Instant alerts are easy to send to healthcare providers for early medical intervention to improve patient outcomes. It will empower predictive maintenance and remote monitoring solutions in the pharmaceutical and healthcare sectors through IoT with AI and ML.This approach ensures the reliability of medical equipment and pharmaceutical production and enhances patient care and safety.

3.7 AI/ML for Patient Monitoring and Signal Analysis

A modern healthcare method using AI/ML technology is the Remote Patient Monitoring (RPM). It enables the tracking of patients at home outside the traditional clinical settings. The health data of the patient is collected and transferred to healthcare team in real time for in-time interventions and the personalized care. For example, the wearable devices are used to monitor the conditions like blood pressure, heart rate and activity level, if the patient is diagnosed with hypertension. The device collects data daily and sends it to a secure cloud platform.

- ***Data Collection:*** The patient wears the device daily, collects their vital signs regularly and creates a data stream.
- ***Data Transmission:*** Data is securely transmitted to a cloud-based platform using wireless technology or a smartphone app and the data is aggregated with other patients.
- ***AI and ML Analysis***: AI algorithms and ML models analyse the data in real-time, detecting patterns, anomalies and trends. For example, individuals or HCPs (Health Care Professionals) may notice a steady increase in a patient's blood pressure at any time as needed.
- ***Alerts and Insights:*** AI can triggers alerts to the health provider in case of concerning patterns or deviations. For example, if a patient's blood pressure remains too high for a long time, a warning is issued of possible hypertension.
- ***Interventions and treatments:*** The healthcare provider can proactively intervene by adjusting medication, suggesting lifestyle changes, or scheduling follow-ups.
- ***Continuous monitoring and optimisation:*** Remote Patient Monitoring (RPM) allows tracking and improvement. It formulates treatment plans, optimises medication use and plans individual care based on long-term trends.

AI and ML continuously monitor critical parameters for real-time analysis to ensure timely intervention for remote optimisation. This means a better prognosis, fewer in-person visits & hospitalisations and better health outcomes and efficiency. For example, Cure App and LYFE.

Signal analysis in health sciences deals with data that change over time or space. Common examples of physiological signals are found in the health sciences. With the advent of AI and ML in healthcare, signal analysis has been revolutionised. Large datasets are being processed in real-time and patterns, irregularities and trends can quickly detected. These technologies can capture unexpected changes in a patient's vital signs and indicate the onset of certain medical conditions that require intervention. Signal analysis work is mentioned below:

- **Data acquisition:** The process of data collection by sensors, instruments, or devices to measure various physiological signals (such as heart rate, blood pressure, or activity level), using wearable monitors.
- **Preprocessing:** The process of filtering noise, removing artefacts and correcting baseline drift are used for cleaning and enhancing the data.
- **Feature extraction:** The process of extracting relevant features/ characteristics from preprocessed data, like peaks, valleys, frequency components and statistical measures etc.
- **Analysis with interpretation:** The patterns, trends, anomalies, or correlations using statistical methods, time-frequency analysis, spectral analysis, or AI/ML algorithms, are examined using extracted features.
- **Interpretation and Decision Making:** The interpretation are made in the healthcare context and analyze the results to diagnose diseases, track health, predict outcomes and inform medical decisions.

Signal analysis enables healthcare professionals to diagnose patients better, predict their outcomes and develop personalised treatment plans. It helps in the intelligent use of resources, sound decision-making and early problem detection, improving patient care and streamlining healthcare systems.

3.8 AI/ML Transformation in Pharmaceuticals with Robotics

The introduction of robotics and automation has brought about the most significant changes in the pharmaceutical industry. These changes have resulted from advances in AI and ML. Robotics and automation, combined with AI/ML technologies, constantly transform the pharmaceutical industry by increasing efficiency, reducing costs, ensuring quality and fostering innovation in drug discovery and formulation development. Some modern applications of AI/ML in robotics and automation related to the pharmaceutical sector are shown in Figure 3.3.

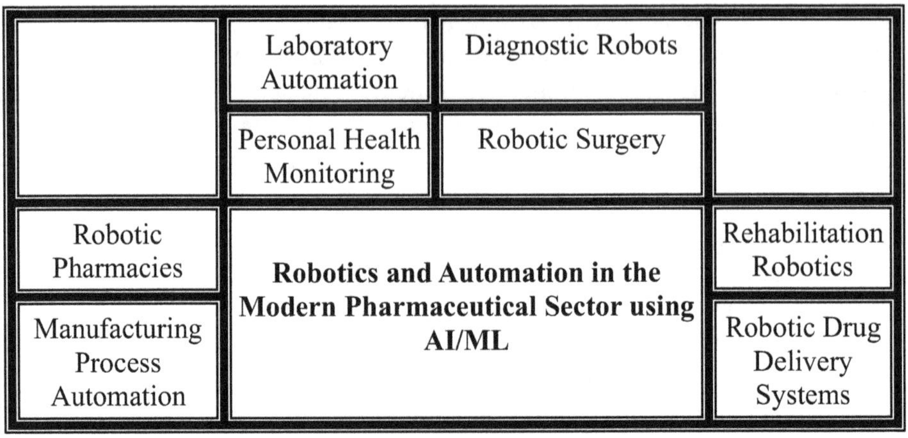

Figure 3.3 Robotics and Automation in the Modern Pharmaceutical Sector with AI/ML.

- **Laboratory automation:** The use of robots and automated systems to perform laboratory tasks such as handling samples, mixing liquids and conducting tests. For example, a robotic arm could accurately pipette small amounts of liquids into test tubes, reducing human error and increasing efficiency.
- **Diagnostic robots:** These are robots that perform diagnostic tasks, such as analysing medical images or testing patient samples. For example, a diagnostic robot can be programmed to examine X-rays for bone fractures or tumours, allowing doctors to make more accurate and timely diagnoses.
- **Personal health monitoring:** These devices and systems use robotics and AI/ML to monitor a person's health at home or *'on the go'*. For example, wearable devices can monitor heart rate and activity levels and alert the user and their healthcare provider to any abnormalities.
- **Robotic pharmacy:** An automated pharmacy system that dispenses medication manages inventory and provides patient consultation. For example, a robotic pharmacy system accurately counts and packages pills, reducing the risk of errors and freeing pharmacists from mundane tasks so they can focus on patient care.
- **Robotic surgery:** This type of surgery uses robots to assist surgeons in more precise and controllable procedures. For example, a surgical robot will make small incisions to position the patient. At the same time, minimally invasive surgery, such as tumor removal or tissue restoration, causes less pain at the patient's wound site and allows for faster recovery.

- **Manufacturing process automation:** The robots and automated systems are used to streamline pharmaceutical production from drug preparation to packaging. To ensure consistency and quality in each batch produced, a pharmaceutical company may use robotic arms to fill vials with precisely measured amounts of a drug.
- **Rehabilitation Robotics:** These are robots designed to assist in the rehabilitation process for individuals recovering from injuries or surgeries. An example could be a robotic exoskeleton that helps patients regain mobility and strength after a stroke or spinal cord injury, guiding them through targeted exercises and movements.
- **Robotic Drug Dispensing Systems:** These systems use robots to deliver medications to patients, either internally or externally. For example, Vejthani Hospital in Thailand has integrated pharmacy robotic dispensing systems, such as 'EV220' for outpatient and 'PROUD' for inpatient services. These robots accurately dispense medications, reducing errors and improving patient safety. These robots are connected to the hospital's information system, streamline the process and alert staff when stocks are low. This advancement ensures faster, safer medication management and meets international standards.

Full automation involves collecting process performance data, analysing it through cloud-connected technology, employing AI-based algorithms to derive knowledge and using this knowledge to improve process control. Automation addresses quality issues, human errors, manual manufacturing inconsistencies, cost pressures and global competition in the medical manufacturing sector. It is undeniable that AI and ML are revolutionising the pharmaceutical industry, particularly when combined with robotics. With the incorporation of AI, ML and robotics, the pharmaceutical industry is positioned to make significant paces in drug discovery, development, manufacturing and patient care.

3.9 AI/ML- Driven Wearable Technology and Biosensors

Wearable technology monitors various activities such as vital signs, assists in illness detection and supports patient health monitoring, including the care of aged population. Recent medical sensors and electronic chip miniaturisation advancements have expanded wearable technology applications. Different kinds of wearable devices and their applications are shown in Table 3.5.

Table 3.5 Wearable Devices and Their Applications.

Sr. No.	Wearable Device	Application
1	Glucose Monitor	Glucose level estimations regularly done by a Continuous Glucose Monitor (CGM) records over time. These monitor use various methods to show and store the data. Some CGMs automatically transmit and show information to the smartphone or receiver.
2	Body Temperature and Activity tracking sensor	Healthcare facilities are using more and more wearable motion trackers, which continuously detect the user's movement in real-time. They can encourage users to exercise more while giving them feedback on their performance.
3	Blood Oxygen Monitoring Sensor	A Pulse Oximeter is a popular oxygen saturation monitoring tool in medical settings for non-invasively measuring and examining blood oxygen saturation levels.
4	Transcutaneous Electrical Nerve Stimulation (TENS) therapy devices	Low-voltage electrical currents are used in Transcutaneous Electrical Nerve Stimulation (TENS) to reduce pain. Medical professionals use TENS to treat various ailments like osteoarthritis, tendonitis and fibromyalgia.
5	Insulin Pumps	Insulin pumps are compact electronic gadgets. They resemble miniature cell phones in size. On a pre-set schedule, insulin pumps administer dosages of the drug and blood sugar is regulated.
6	Electro Cardio Gram (ECG) Patches	Patients can wear the new discretely worn patches that use wireless data transmission. Some of these gadgets also include more sophisticated features, such as the capacity to track skin temperature and breathing.
7	Implanted Cardioverter Defibrillator (ICD)	A tiny battery-operated device called an Implanted Cardioverter-Defibrillator (ICD) is inserted into the chest. Arrhythmias, commonly known as irregular heartbeats, are found and stopped by it. An ICD continuously monitors the heartbeat. It administers electric shocks to help the heart return to a normal rhythm when necessary.

Devices range from watches to prosthetics, which form the part of Internet of Medical Things (IoMT) and often connect to mobile devices. Various sensors like thermometers and accelerometers continually monitor human signals, although some may lack precision compared to hospital equipment. ML algorithms extract valuable patterns from sensor data, like notifications on the Apple Watch and Eko's heart murmur detection algorithm. The intersection of healthcare, technology and data science is being reshaped by AI/ML-driven wearable technologies and biosensors. These devices utilise advanced AI and ML models to analyse data collected from sensors worn on or inside the body, offering valuable insights into health and well-being. AI/ML is transforming wearable technologies and biosensors:

- Personalised health monitoring is enabled by AI/ML algorithms, which analyse continuous streams of biometric data from wearable sensors to provide tailored health insights. Stress, fatigue, or irregularities in heart rate can be detected, assisting individuals in proactively managing their health.
- AI/ML-powered wearables enable remote patient monitoring, allowing physicians to monitor patients with chronic diseases or recovering from surgery and alert them to any deterioration for early intervention.
- Predictive healthcare analytics, powered by AI/ML, is crucial in improving healthcare resource allocation. Collecting large amounts of data from a variety of sources, such as wearable devices and using it to trend population health and predict disease outbreaks ensures that resources are optimally distributed, thereby improving the efficiency of the healthcare system.
- Wearable devices equipped with biosensors and AI/ML can manage severe conditions like diabetes, heart disease and respiratory disorders with continuous real-time monitoring of chronic diseases. ML algorithms process physiological parameters to generate early warnings of potential health complications and allow timely intervention.
- Wearable devices powered by AI/ML provide fitness tracking and improve performance by analysing movement patterns, heart rate variability and other biometric data to tailor workout plans, prevent injuries and optimise training regimens.
- AI/ML algorithms enable personalised recommendations, contextual feedback and device settings optimisation based on usage patterns, all of which is improving the user experience.

Biosensors are devices that detect biological substances, enzymes or Deoxyribonucleic Acid (DNA) and convert the result into an electrical or optical signal. Biosensors have applications in health care, environmental monitoring and food safety assurance. All biosensors consist of a biological detection element, an enzyme and a transducer that converts the biological response into an electrical or optical signal. Biosensors with AI/ML accelerate health care. In other words, the complex data generated by biosensors integrated with AI and ML are now able to analyse more effectively to aid in accurate diagnosis, better health monitoring and the development of new point-of-care devices. AI and ML are being used with biosensors as mentioned below:

- **Extraction of meaningful data:** AI/ML algorithms mine the large amounts of data produced by biosensors. They can identify patterns and thus provide precious insights that would otherwise go unnoticed by traditional methods. For example, a biosensor continuously monitors a diabetic patient's blood sugar level. ML algorithms analyse trends and predict the likelihood of hypoglycemic or hyperglycemic events for the patient, thereby avoiding such situations.
- **Personalised medicine:** AI/ML uses unique biosensor data, medical history and genetics to develop a customised treatment plan and prevention strategy. For example, a wearable biosensor continuously monitors heart function. The AI analyses data to identify patterns that indicate a higher risk of arrhythmia based on the patient's medical history.
- **Increased diagnostic accuracy:** AI/ML compares biosensor data to large medical databases to provide more accurate diagnoses with lower error rates. For example, an AI-enabled alcohol breathalyser detects not only alcohol consumption but also underlying health conditions that may cause an increase in specific breath components.
- **Point-of-Care Diagnostics:** AI/ML-enabled biosensors are readily portable, easy to use and allow on-the-spot diagnosis, independent of a benchtop laboratory or expensive testing equipment. For example, a smartphone attachment biosensor analyses a finger-prick blood sample. It uses AI to detect the presence of specific pathogens, enabling rapid diagnosis of infectious diseases in remote areas.

AI/ML-driven wearable technologies and biosensors constantly revolutionise healthcare by enabling continuous monitoring, personalised interventions and data-driven insights for improved health outcomes.

3.10 AI/ML in Pharmaceutical Supply Chain Management

Many industries are making progress to meet customer demands and expectations through different methodologies. The pharmaceutical sector, which is crucial for saving lives had faced challenges during the COVID-19 pandemic. The global biopharmaceutical supply chain was impacted, affecting sourcing raw materials and distributing finished products. Supply chain disruptions arise from various factors such as pandemics, natural disasters, pricing changes, cyberattacks, logistical delays and product issues. Transportation challenges induced by the epidemic have affected the supply chain network and global industries.

The various interconnected steps are the part of supply chain, which aid in the development, production, distribution and delivery of pharmaceutical/biopharmaceutical products. These steps are research and development, clinical trials, regulatory approvals, manufacturing, labelling, packaging, distribution, warehousing, inventory management, cold chain management, regulatory compliance and post market surveillance.

The process of discovering, developing and improving the new drugs/biologics, repurposing of existing drug relates to the research and development step. The safety and efficacy studies following initial preclinical studies and human trials are used to evaluate the drug candidates during the clinical trial step. The data developed during clinical trial phase is reviewed by the regulatory agencies and further approve the products for entry into the market. The complex process involves the cell culture, fermentation, purification and packaging for the manufacturing of the product. The strict quality control standards must be following during this step. The products are further packed and labelled as the country's regulatory requirements in order to ensure that the product integrity and process compliance.

The efficient delivering of finished products and the compliance of regulatory standards is also the point of care. The products may require special storage conditions. The product quality and safety can easily be ensured by providing the storage facilities adhering to regulatory requirements. To meet the market demand of product and to minimize the excess inventory associated cost, the inventory levels are managed. The orders are taken and filled by automation or by human intervention. The product stability during transportation and storage (for vaccines and biologics) require cold chain management.

The industry must ensure compliance with supply chain regulations such as Good Manufacturing Practices (GMP), Current Good Manufacturing Practices (cGMP), Good Distribution Practices (GDP) and others for quality, safety and efficacy. Post-marketing surveillance (PMS) activities continue to ensure product safety. Safety and provisions for adverse events or other safety concerns that arise after the product is released to the market are directly related to PMS. Each step in the pharmaceutical supply chain, from initial research and development to product delivery and post-market surveillance, positively contributes to ensuring the availability and safety of biopharmaceutical products. Organisations need to address several significant challenges for big data to transform the pharmaceutical supply chain truly. Key challenges within pharmaceutical supply chain management include:

- Cold chain management necessitates strict temperature control and handling throughout the process.
- Ensuring the highest quality and repeatability in drug manufacturing.
- Fragmented multimodal networks.
- Issues related to drug counterfeiting.
- Lack of end-to-end visibility.
- Personalised treatment demands, such as T-cell therapy for specific patients.
- Strict deadlines.
- Manufacturing issues.
- Expensive procedures and other requirements.

AI and ML allow the continual transformation of the pharmaceutical supply chain, making it more efficient, safe and cost-effective by addressing specific difficulties that become critical to successful integration. AI and ML technologies are altering the pharmaceutical supply chain, making it efficient, accurate and inventive steps at various levels:

1. **Improve safety and quality control (QC):** The technologies based on AI/ML such as image recognition and sensor technology are used to ensure the quality and safety of medicines at all stages of the supply chain.
2. **Improved efficiency:** The operations like, inventory management, shipping, delivery, production are optimized using AI and ML tools.
3. **Industrial:** The industrial processes, eliminating the waste and increasing the efficiency can easily be optimized by AI/ML technology. Error-free automation may become possible in the future.
4. **Inventory management:** The past data and current trends are used by predictive algorithms to optimise inventory levels, ensuring that pharmaceuticals are available, when needed.

5. **Shipping and delivery:** The algorithms optimise the route to ensure that patients get their medications on time. The various factors such as traffic and weather conditions are considered by algorithm.

The inventory management in the pharmaceutical business by optimising stock levels, eliminating waste and ensuring the timely availability of essential medicines is improved by AI/ML tools. These innovations significantly increase forecasting accuracy, reducing the risk of stock outs and overstocks. The advantages of AI/ML in pharmaceutical inventory management are:

- **Cost Limitation:** The integration of AI/ML with inventory management software in a pharmaceutical company helps to reduce costs by optimising inventory, reducing excess storage and preventing stock-out situations. The overstocking of expensive medications by accurately forecasting demand and streamlining inventory replenishment processes can be avoided, resulting in cost savings.
- **Data-driven insights:** The vast amounts of data generated within pharmaceutical inventory management systems can provide actionable insights and intelligence using AI/ML algorithms. This advanced analytics help the companies to understand inventory trends, customer preferences and market dynamics and make data-driven decisions on optimising inventory levels, pricing strategies and product offerings.
- **Higher Efficiency:** AI/ML-powered inventory management software are able to streamline processes and workflows, thereby increasing the efficiency manifold across the entire pharmaceutical supply chain. The reduction in lead times, elimination of delays and optimisation of operations can help the companies to improve speed and responsiveness with fewer tasks such as inventory monitoring, order fulfilment and supplier management.
- **Enhanced Accessibility:** AI/ML inventory management software improves accessibility by allowing real-time visibility of inventory levels, transactions and supply chain activities from any device. The stakeholders can access critical inventory information from any location at any time with cloud based solution and mobile application, leading to faster decision-making, more efficient collaboration and better responsiveness to change the market conditions or other unexpected situations.
- **Error Reduction:** The errors and inaccuracies are eliminated by automating routine tasks and incorporating advanced validation mechanisms by AI/ML inventory management system. It eliminates manual entry errors, miscounts and discrepancies, protects data

integrity and encourages regulatory compliance to improve inventory accuracy. It also reduces the potential for highly costly errors and operational disruptions.

- **Higher Productivity:** The inventory management pharmaceutical software empowered with AI/ML algorithms can significantly improve the productivity by automating repetitive tasks such as inventory tracking, order processing and forecasting. This also frees up some valuable human resources to focus on higher-level tasks, thereby increasing overall operational efficiency.

AI, ML, automation and robotics increasingly support the pharmaceutical industry. It also helps in software development, data transfer, computing, etc. In pharmaceuticals, AI and ML are used for tasks like drugs, medical device software and patient monitoring. Wearable devices equipped with AI algorithms are also being developed to monitor patients with serious illnesses remotely. Many pharmaceutical companies have already developed products and services associated with AI and ML algorithms that can remotely monitor patients suffering from life-threatening diseases. These advancements are constantly revolutionising the sector and addressing significant challenges through innovative solutions.

Proposed Questions

Long Answer Type Questions (10 Marks Each)

1. Describe the role of AI/ML in optimising healthcare supply chain and inventory management processes.
2. Explain the role of pharmacists in the modern pharmaceutical sector, particularly in light of technological advancements such as AI/ML and digital therapeutics.
3. Enumerate the applications of AI/ML in medical imaging and analysis, highlighting its significance in modern healthcare.
4. Discuss the utilisation of wearable technology and biosensors in the pharmaceutical sector.
5. How are robotics and automation integrated into the modern pharmaceutical sector through AI/ML technologies?
6. How do AI/ML technologies enhance the efficiency and effectiveness of healthcare supply chain operations?
7. How does AI/ML-based software function as a medical device and what are its implications in the pharmaceutical sector?

8. What is the significance of AI/ML in diagnosing medical conditions and how does it contribute to improved healthcare outcomes? Discuss briefly.
9. What role does AI/ML play in predictive maintenance and remote monitoring within the pharmaceutical industry?
10. What are the key roles of artificial intelligence (AI) and machine learning (ML) in the pharmaceutical sector and why are they considered essential?

Short Answer Type Questions (5 Marks Each)

1. Provide the examples of FDA-approved medical devices that utilise AI/ML technology and how do they enhance patient care?
2. Explain the role of AI and ML-driven wearable technology and biosensors in healthcare and how are they revolutionising patient care and monitoring?
3. Discuss the importance of AI/ML in patient monitoring and physiological signal analysis, emphasising its benefits for healthcare providers.
4. How are AI and ML being used in medical imaging and analysis to improve diagnostic accuracy and patient outcomes?
5. How are AI/ML-based medical devices transforming various aspects of healthcare, including patient monitoring, medical imaging and predictive maintenance?
6. How are robotics being integrated into the pharmaceutical sector through AI and ML technologies and what advantages do they offer in terms of efficiency and precision?
7. How do AI and ML contribute to patient monitoring and signal analysis and what impact do these technologies have on early detection and intervention in healthcare?
8. How does the Internet of Medical Things (IoMT) contribute to advancements in the pharmaceutical sector and what are its primary applications?
9. How are AI and ML being utilised in pharmaceutical supply chain management to improve efficiency, reduce costs and ensure product quality and safety?
10. What are digital therapeutics (DTx) and how do they differ from traditional pharmaceutical treatments? How are AI and ML being integrated into DTx?

11. What are some examples of AI and ML applications for predictive maintenance and remote monitoring in healthcare settings and how do they benefit healthcare facilities and patients?

Very Short Questions (1 Mark)

1. What is IoMT and its impact on the pharmaceutical sector?
2. Why is AI/ML important in the pharmaceutical sector?
3. How do pharmacists contribute to the modern pharmaceutical sector?
4. Name any two FDA-approved AI/ML medical devices.
5. How does DTx use AI/ML?
6. How does AI/ML enhance medical imaging?
7. What does AI/ML do for predictive maintenance?
8. How does AI/ML improve patient monitoring?
9. How are robotics changing pharmaceuticals with AI/ML?
10. What benefits do AI/ML-driven wearables offer?
11. How does AI/ML optimise pharmaceutical supply chains?

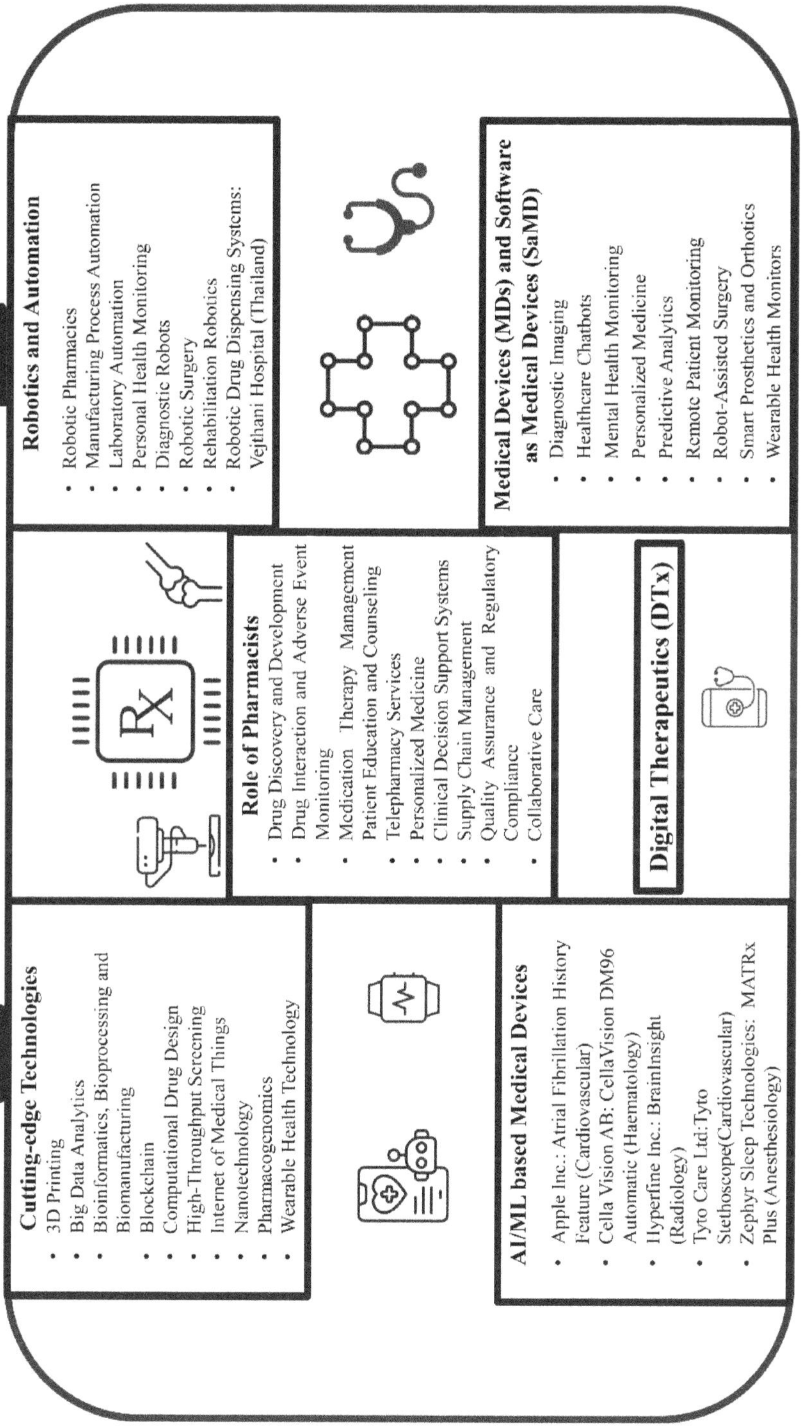
AI
Modern Pharmaceutical Sector
ML
Cutting-edge Technologies
3D Printing
Big Data Analytics
Bioinformatics, Bioprocessing and Biomanufacturing
Blockchain
Computational Drug Design
High-Throughput Screening
Internet of Medical Things
Nanotechnology
Pharmacogenomics
Wearable Health Technology
Rx
Robotics and Automation
Robotic Pharmacies
Manufacturing Process Automation
Laboratory Automation
Personal Health Monitoring
Diagnostic Robots
Robotic Surgery
Rehabilitation Robotics
Robotic Drug Dispensing Systems: Vejthani Hospital (Thailand)
Role of Pharmacists
Drug Discovery and Development
Drug Interaction and Adverse Event Monitoring
Medication Therapy Management
Patient Education and Counseling
Telepharmacy Services
Personalized Medicine
Clinical Decision Support Systems
Supply Chain Management
Quality Assurance and Regulatory Compliance
Collaborative Care
AI/ML based Medical Devices
Apple Inc.: Atrial Fibrillation History Feature (Cardiovascular)
Cella Vision AB: CellaVision DM96 Automatic (Haematology)
Hyperfine Inc.: BrainInsight (Radiology)
Tyto Care Ltd:Tyto Stethoscope(Cardiovascular)
Zephyr Sleep Technologies: MATRx Plus (Anesthesiology)
Digital Therapeutics (DTx)
Medical Devices (MDs) and Software as Medical Devices (SaMD)
Diagnostic Imaging
Healthcare Chatbots
Mental Health Monitoring
Personalized Medicine
Predictive Analytics
Remote Patient Monitoring
Robot-Assisted Surgery
Smart Prosthetics and Orthotics
Wearable Health Monitors

CHAPTER 4

AI and ML in Clinical Care and Healthcare Operations

4.1 Introduction

Artificial Intelligence (AI) and Machine Learning (ML), Deep learning (DL), three-dimensional (3D) printing, robotics, are some of the technologies constantly revolutionizing the digital healthcare sector with different innovations. AI, ML and DL significantly contribute to developing advanced health systems in many health-related domains, such as diagnostics, patient information and records management and disorder treatment. These technologies offer different innovations associated with the healthcare sector and they even offer many opportunities to reduce human error, enhance treatment outcomes and collect data over extended periods. Improved patient care, medical Research and Development (R&D) are based on the ongoing integration of technology into all healthcare aspects.

Under current circumstances, AI and ML are continuously contributing to the clinical evaluation of drugs, devices and software or combinations thereof. Advanced technologies (AI/ML/DL) are streamlining the development process in the modern era to facilitate clinical care and various healthcare operations, such as clinical trials, virtual clinical trials, decentralized clinical trials and many more.

4.2 AI and ML for Diagnostics and Prognosis

The Health Care Professionals (HCPs) are utilizing the AI/ML-enabled tools for the purpose of precise diagnosis of diseases by evaluating symptoms, patient histories, laboratory reports and other relevant information. These AI/ML algorithms evaluate the data of medical images such as X-rays, Computed Tomography (CT) scans, Magnetic Resonance Imaging (MRI) scans etc. for identifying anomalies and diagnosing conditions. AI and ML-enabled international standard-based diagnosis tools are crucial for recommending possible healthcare treatment courses based on the available information.

In prognosis, AI/ML models can easily evaluate the various forms of patient data, such as medicinal history, therapy responses and demographics. In addition, it also considers other factors to predict the path of disease and scope of treatment for better outcomes. This assists HCPs in creating better treatment plans and healthcare interventions based on anticipated outcomes. AI/ML-based systems also play a fundamental role in detecting and predicting certain diseases or disorders by reviewing patient history, lifestyle information and genetic information. This AI and ML-based system recommend preventive measures to be adopted much earlier. These tools can also automate basic diagnostic procedures, saving physician's time for more complex conditions. There is also the ability to analyse the data in all critical situations. The applications of AI and ML in diagnostics and prognosis are shown in Figure 4.1.

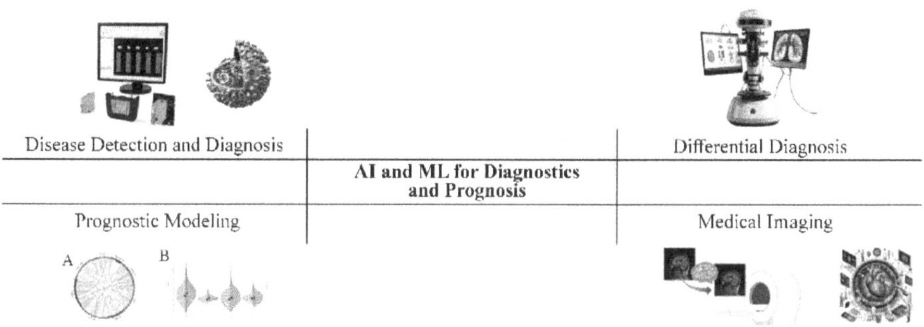

Figure 4.1 Applications of AI and ML in Diagnostics and Prognosis.

- ***Disease Detection and Diagnosis:*** The large amounts of patient data, including medical history, symptoms and laboratory results, are processed by AI models to assist healthcare providers in diagnosing the diseases. AI's ability to recognise patterns in complex data sets can lead to quicker and more accurate diagnoses. AI algorithms developed by computer professionals proposed for detecting and diagnosing diseases such as cancer, lung diseases, rheumatoid arthritis, diabetic retinopathy, heart diseases, Alzheimer's disease, hepatitis, dengue, liver disease, Parkinson's disease and many more.
- ***Differential Diagnosis:*** AI and ML can assist in distinguishing between different diseases or conditions with similar symptoms, helping clinicians to make more accurate diagnoses. For example, artificial intelligence and ultrasound data can be utilised to differentiate between tiny breast phyllodes tumours and fibroadenomas. ML approaches are also employed for the differential diagnosis of jaundice detection using colour-corrected smartphone images and various other skin diseases.

- ***Medical Imaging:*** AI/ML is revolutionising radiology and medical diagnostics by analysing and interpreting medical images such as X-rays, CT scans MRIs, ultrasounds and pathology slides to detect and diagnose diseases early. For example, ML analysis of brain MRI can detect a narrow time frame from symptom onset to tissue changes, indicating early ischemic stroke with greater sensitivity than a human reader. Similarly, AI models for heart structure segmentation also include tracking microscopic abnormal traces.
- ***Prognostic Modelling:*** AI and Ml-based prediction models can easily provide the patient prognosis based on available clinical data and patient history. The early prognosis assists in treatment planning and patient counselling during all the stages. For example, computer-aided diagnosis (CAD) tools are handy for pathologists as these tools support the diagnosis of diseases like leukaemia. The most precise and accurate CAD system for Acute Myeloid Leukaemia (AML) can be developed using White Blood Cells (WBC) fragmentation data. Similarly, AI and ML can be helpful in the diagnosis of Cardiovascular Diseases (CVD) like arrhythmias, angiography and fetal health, among many others by using data mining techniques.

In the healthcare sector, the integration of AI and ML algorithms led to the advancement of diagnosis and prognosis up to a large extent. The case study mentioned below highlights how AI and ML assist in improving diagnosis and prognosis with a primary aim of improving the outcomes of patients with Cardio Vascular Disease (CVD).

Case Study Scenario: A hospital is actively trying to quickly and accurately establish cardiac disease patients' prognosis and diagnosis patterns. The administration approach is to optimize resource utilization for better patient outcomes. Through the application of AI and Ml technology, the hospital has implemented the following necessary steps towards better healthcare outcomes:

- ***Data collection and integration:*** It involves the collection and integration of patient datasets, such as medical imaging scans, Electronic Health Records (EHRs), laboratory results, genetic information and many others. The centralized data repository has the availability of standardized datasets.
- ***Feature Engineering:*** The relevant features are required by AI and ML algorithms for accurate analysis leading to better outcomes. Data scientist are helping the HCPs to identify key features from the integrated dataset, including blood pressure readings, cholesterol levels, imaging characteristics, patient demographics etc.

- ***Model/Algorithm Development:*** The creation and trainings of AI and ML algorithms is performed by data scientist using curated datasets. The diagnostic algorithms (to detect the presence of cardiovascular disease) and prediction algorithms (to predict the risk of future cardiovascular events) are included in this step.
- ***Model testing and validation:*** The developed models are evaluated for performance metrics (accuracy, sensitivity, specificity and area under the receiver operating characteristic curve) and rigorous validation. The cross-validation techniques are also applied to ensure its performance in larger patient populations.
- ***Clinical workflow integration:*** The validated AI/ML models are further integrated into the hospital's clinical workflow. These models are utilized by the HCPs through user-friendly interfaces that have been built into their hospitals' Electronic Medical Record (EMR) systems. The real-time diagnostic support and prognostic information to clinical decision-making are the main features of the AI/ML models.

According to implementation, the results and benefits are the following:

- ***Better accuracy:*** The significant impact of AI and ML models is the diagnostic accuracy, which is much higher than traditional methods. It results in earlier detection of cardiovascular disease.
- ***Improved prognosis:*** The predictive models are applied by the HCPs to identify high-risk patients and provide early intervention. It helps to provide preventive measures and personalised treatment plans (if required) to reduce the incidence of adverse cardiovascular events.
- ***Increased efficiency:*** Process automation of diagnostic workflows and decision support tools accelerates clinical workflow, allowing healthcare providers to focus on genuinely providing patient care.
- ***Cost Reduction:*** This saves money for patients and healthcare systems, as AI and ML prevent many unnecessary diagnostic tests and hospitalisations caused by cardiovascular disease and its avoidable complications.

The AI and ML technologies are successfully integrated with diagnosis and prognosis in hospital settings point to new possibilities in healthcare delivery. Similarly, harnessing the power of data-driven insights to connect healthcare providers improves patient outcomes, operational efficiency and cost-effectiveness when dealing with complex medical conditions like heart disease. Some significant examples of AI and ML for diagnosis and prognosis are mentioned below:

- LuminairesCore, developed by Digital Diagnostics, is an AI-based diagnostic system for detecting Diabetic Retinopathy (DR) and Diabetic Macular Edema (DME) using retinal images obtained during a diabetic eye examination. The Food and Drug Administration (FDA) had approved the autonomous AI system, which provides diagnosis at the point of care without needing specialised interpretation, increasing the efficiency and accessibility of care for diabetes patients.

- SkinVision is the first mobile app based on AI and ML helping consumers to identify spots and moles on the skin prone to skin cancer, specifically melanoma. Machine learning algorithms analyse photographs of skin lesions submitted by users for examination and dermatologists review of the images for accuracy. This technology is certified with the CE mark as a regulated medical device, thus reliable and safe. SkinVision assesses skin cancer risk, recommends next steps and tracks changes in moles over time. It aids early detection but does not replace professional diagnosis by a dermatologist despite having a high assessment accuracy rate. However, misdiagnosis cannot be avoided.
- Subtle Medical is a healthcare technology company that pioneered the use of AI in medical imaging procedures. SubtlePET and SubtleMR use AI algorithms to process images from PET and MR scanning devices. SubtlePET reduces PET scan time by up to four times while maintaining image quality, while SubtleMR improves both image quality and MR scan time. Subtle Medical's solutions help to accelerate scan times while maintaining diagnostic accuracy, resulting in a faster, safer and wiser imaging practice for patients and healthcare providers.
- Qure.ai Technologies Private Limited uses AI to improve healthcare accessibility and affordability. Quri.ai have various products and services associated with AI and ML are:
    - qXR detects multiple chest abnormalities swiftly, including lung and heart issues. qXR is certified by CE MDR Class IIB and approved by FDA.
    - qXR-HF aids in the early detection of heart failure risk with real-time notifications.
    - The qLC suite offers qCT for chest CT scans and qXR-LC for chest X-rays to treat lung nodules. QXR-LC detects lung cancer nodules and provides a malignancy risk score and qCT makes it easier to identify and track lung nodules early.

The Qure app facilitates the continuous collaboration and instant image access for quick healthcare reporting in tune with the regulations.

AI and ML in healthcare diagnosis and prognosis are just the beginning of a new revolution in this field. Various innovations and other developments around AI/ML are revolutionising patient care at all stages.

4.3 Electronic Health Records (EHR) with AI/ML Clinical Decision Support (CDS)

The digital representations of paper patient charts having all relevant medical history, diagnoses, prescriptions, test results and other information is known as Electronic Health Records (EHRs). The best possible care is feasible by providing the access of the EHRs to the physician/health care professionals. The accessibility, efficiency, accuracy and interoperability are the benefits of EHRs over the paper records. The EHRs also facilitates exchange of information between all healthcare providers. It ultimately enhances the workflow, reduces the errors, improving patient safety and other health outcomes.

The benefits of integrating AI and ML into EHRs include the better treatment decisions, early disease detection and workflow optimisation, population-level management, continuous learning and improvements in the patient care & health outcomes. Some of the essential aspects related to AI and ML for enhancing EHR systems are:

- ***Data analysis and pattern recognition:*** AI and ML are constantly transforming the EHRs through rapid analysis of large data to determine the key trends and patterns. These patterns and trends help to improve disease management and better healthcare outcomes. In addition, it also finds the hidden correlates to detect the disease early and provide personalised treatment recommendations. AI and ML tools are used to determin the patient subgroups for trailered treatment. At the same time, Natural Language Processing (NLP) ensures the completeness of the patient records by turning unstructured data into structured format to provide fruitful information.
- ***Improved workflow and appointment management:*** AI and ML tools help to manage the appointment workflows, thereby, allow the Health Care Professionals (HCPs) to design a flow, which will enable to provide full attention to the patient. Advancements in AI and ML in medical imaging and diagnostics allow proactive healthcare intervention to ensure timely treatment based on the individual's factors such as history and lifestyle choices. Routine tasks are automated using AI to streamline processes and improve radiology workflow efficiency, resulting in better patient care.
- ***Better clinical decision support:*** AI-powered EHRs provide real-time assistance to healthcare providers by using data analysis and best practices for accurate diagnosis and appropriate treatment plans. ML aids in risk stratification, prioritising care for high-risk patients. AI algorithms further enhance medicines' safety by predicting patients susceptible to potential drug interactions and adverse reactions. For example, platforms like Zebra Medical Vision empower health

providers to detect disease risks immediately and propose preventive treatments that ensure better patient care. The flow chart for AI/ML-based clinical decision support is illustrated in Figure 4.2.

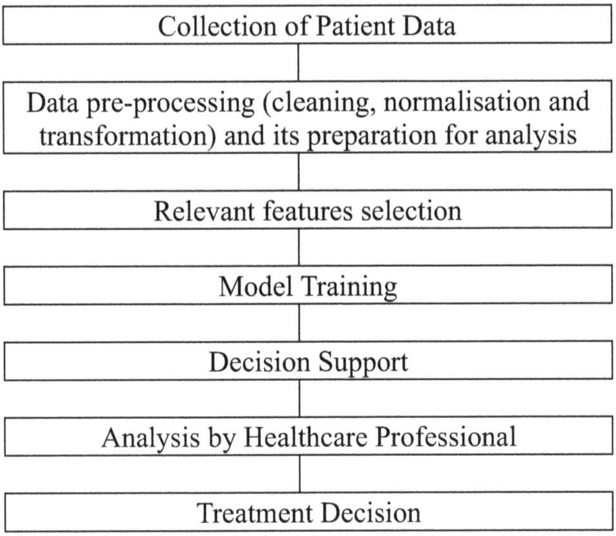

Figure 4.2 Clinical Decision Support Using AI and ML.

Patient data are first acquired, then cleaned, normalised and transformed in preparation for analysis. Later, suitable features are extracted from the prepared data. In the final step of this approach, a model will be trained using these features. This trained model will provide decision support, allowing healthcare providers to base their treatment decisions on the basis of data analysed.

- **Population health management:** AI and ML can analyse large amounts of patient data to discover health patterns, disease prevalence and places where public health intervention is needed.
- **Risk Prediction:** AI helps to predict patients' outcomes, re-admission risks and other complications that may arise, thus allowing healthcare providers to intervene on time with an optimal patient care plan. AI algorithms will sift through drug databases and patient information to detect drug interactions and predict adverse events that can reduce medication errors and increase patient safety. This information will be fed into ML models to predict the likelihood of certain diseases or medical conditions so that appropriate healthcare providers can identify high-risk patients and proactively initiate preventive measures or interventions.
- **Treatment Plan:** Personalized treatment plans are based on each patient's symptoms. The AI/ML tools are utilized to make decisions

based on past medical records and symptoms. The patient data and medical literature are analyzed by the system. In this way, the effectiveness of treatment is maximized while the adverse effects are minimized. The condition-based testing is assisted by AI and ML ensuring that patients with severe conditions should receive timely care in less waiting time.

4.4 AI/ML for Disease Surveillance and Outbreak Decision

The importance of AI/ML applications in disease surveillance and outbreak decision-making has been witnessed during the reported global health emergency caused by the COVID-19 pandemic. The large amount of data from different sources such as social media, EHRs and satellite imagery was assessed to identify trends and potential epidemics in advance.

The mysterious patterns, which analysts generally miss, can be identified by collecting and analyzing data using AI/ML systems. It allows the earlier detection of epidemic and has faster detection times. The predictive models are also developed using AI/ML, which predict future outbreaks of diseases based on information from weather patterns, population density and travel patterns. The allocation of funds to public health professionals for better health outcomes can be decided based on the recommendations of AI/ML models. Some of the applications of AI and ML in disease surveillance and outbreak decision-making are:

- The news broadcasts and social media feeds are continuously monitored. The AI/ML model utilized this information and can provide information regarding potential outbreaks and signs of the disease much earlier than traditional surveillance approaches.
- The data from mobile phones and other digital sources is analyzed using AI/ML for the purpose of contact tracking. This helps in preventive efforts by identifying people who may have been exposed to infectious diseases.
- Outbreak locations and resource requirements are predicted by AI models, enabling more effective resource allocation by public health officials.
- Genetic data from viruses and bacteria is analysed by AI to track drug resistance emergence, aiding in developing new treatments and preventing resistant strain spread.

Some notable real-world examples related to disease surveillance and outbreak decisions associated with AI and ML are:

- The EPIWATCH system is utilised to identify outbreaks at their inception and conduct rapid risk analyses. It is driven by AI and ML, which affect extensive open-source data and generate automated early warnings for epidemics globally. With whole language and geographic information system capabilities, it utilises field epidemiology and epidemic response expertise. EPIWATCH has been demonstrated to detect outbreak signals earlier than traditional laboratory or hospital-based surveillance and can serve as a prompt for investigating early outbreak signals.

- BlueDot is recognised for providing infectious disease intelligence, employing a combination of humans and AI to monitor and analyse disease outbreaks worldwide. This company assists various governments and public health organisations in preparing and responding to emerging threats.

4.5 Resource Allocation and Capacity Planning with AI and ML in Healthcare Sector

The health sector is grappling with optimising resources and implementing effective capacity planning to meet patients' needs and allocate resources efficiently. AI and ML are effective technologies that enhance healthcare administration capacity planning and resource allocation. The capacity planning involves effectively allocating workers, supplies and infrastructure to meet patient demands. Capacity planning in healthcare is estimating future patient numbers and distributing resources to meet the demands. Some important roles of AI and ML in capacitive planning are:

- ***Real-time management of requests:*** AI/ML detects blockages and rearranges resources using real-time patient flow data and resource availability. AI/ML models ensure that the resources are deployed as per the need resulting in the improvement of efficiency.
- ***Schedule Optimisation:*** AI/ML algorithms examine past staffing trends to optimise staff scheduling. An individualised schedule is created by matching personnel's skill sets with patients' requirements. This plan optimises resource allocation efficiency, guarantees appropriate personnel levels at the lowest possible cost and meets new needs.
- ***Predictive analytics:*** To predict upcoming demands, AI/ML algorithms analyse historical patterns of in-patient admissions, duration of stay, resource utilisation and others. This AI and ML model allows medical facilities to proactively deploy staff, beds and equipment to all affected areas as required.

Effective resource allocation is significantly linked to lower costs, better patient care and more efficient healthcare operations. The AI and ML models are gaining importance in planning the various processes to increase healthcare business efficiency in all the manners. Some of the important roles of AI and ML in capability planning processes are as follows:

- ***Demand-based forecasting:*** The prediction of future patient volumes is feasible using the AI & ML models. This prediction is based on the past patterns and external variables. The examples of external variable include the demographics and seasonal variations. The predictions facilitate the healthcare organisations regarding allocation of right resources before the demand increases.
- ***Facility expansion planning:*** The futuristic healthcare needs can be forecasted by the AI/ML models using patient data and demographic trends. This data can be used by the health care professionals in meeting the increasing demand and making the strategic plans to enhance/expand the facilities.
- ***Bed Management:*** AI/ML algorithms are successful in maximise bed utilisation by predicting the discharge times. The waiting times of the patients has been decreased through bed management optimisation. This effective management has also been witnessed during COVID-19 and now a day, many of the hospitals are following the bed management through these tools.

In healthcare facilities, efficient capacity planning reduces wait times, improves patient access and increases operational effectiveness. In the fight against COVID-19, most countries, including the UK and India, have used hospital capacity planning systems based on AI and ML. These systems use real-time data to forecast and assign patient loads. They acquire knowledge of effective resource management. For example, various governments set up an integrated command and control centre during COVID-19 to monitor COVID-related data in real-time. Through this command centre, officials monitor data regarding hospitals, ICU beds, oxygen availability, medicines and other requirements. This monitoring helps them to make better decisions.

4.6 AI and ML in Clinical Evaluation of Drugs, Devices and Software

Clinical evaluation is the ongoing process of creating, collecting, analysing and evaluating clinical data to ensure that healthcare interventions meet safety and performance standards. The health ecosystem must demonstrate that these interventions are safe, effective and beneficial for patients and the healthcare system. AI and ML bring significant changes to the drug evaluation process. Clinical evaluation of drugs is also interlinked with efficacy and potential risks and how they relate to other types of treatments. Before AI and ML algorithms can be implemented in healthcare practices, especially clinical assessment, they must undergo adequate evaluation in all aspects to enhance patient safety, efficiency and security.

Clinical evaluation should ensure that AI/ML performs satisfactorily through external testing and demonstrate the benefits of AI/ML-assisted care over traditional methods using well-designed studies with comparisons. Ideally, these should be prospective studies. The landscape of clinical assessment with AI/ML is rapidly changing, creating opportunities to develop new treatments with greater efficiency and accuracy, thereby promoting personalised medicine. The search for suitable drug candidates had been time-consuming and expensive using traditional methods/approaches. AI and ML, on the other hand, can scan large data repositories in search of potential therapeutic molecules, making them promising newcomers to accelerate drug discovery. Trial design can be optimized with AI and ML to determine the ideal dose, patient demographics and key performance indicators, including clinical trial endpoints. This can reduce the time required for drug development, while increasing the possibility of meaningful results.

AI and ML demonstrate remarkable efficacy in handling complex data produced during clinical trials. The subtle patterns and trends are revealed which remain obscure using traditional techniques. This increases knowledge about the drug's therapeutic potential and provides early warning about its risks. AI/ML models enable dynamic modifications to trial protocols and personalized treatments by predicting real-time treatment responses and disease progression. Tasks related to data administration, storage and analyses are automated by AI and ML, which reduces mistakes and increases testing accessibility. By gathering patterns and insights from massive datasets, machine learning algorithms provide important conclusions for decision-making. Understanding long-term outcomes in more diverse patient populations than those observed in controlled contexts requires using Real-World Evidence (RWE). Beyond clinical trials; AI/ML can process data from electronic health records and other sources to provide insightful analysis. Platforms like Data Robot, significantly impacting the ethical standards and transparency of AI-driven clinical research, incorporate fairness-aware algorithms and model interpretation techniques.

4.7 AI & ML in Clinical Development: Real-World Patient Data Analysis

Real-world evidence (RWE) provides fundamental clinical insights based on data from real-world settings such as EHRs, insurance claims and patient registries. Unlike controlled clinical trials, RWE collects information from various sources, including mobile devices and patient-provided or contributed data. It is helpful for regulatory bodies to make decisions on the use of new medicines and monitor the safety of medicine after it's availability in the market. For healthcare providers, RWE provides a better understanding of how treatments work in real life, which allows for better patient care and updated clinical guidelines. The use of real-world data also informs policy-making and improves general healthcare delivery. The use of AI and ML in clinical, Real-World Evidence (RWE) and patient data analytics is a paradigm shift. The major points of concern are:

- ***Clinical trial optimisation:*** AI/ML algorithms optimise many aspects of trials. Historical data analysis can also be used in patient selection and protocol design. Platforms like TriNetX match patients with trials, thus making recruitment easier.
- ***Drug discovery and repurposing:*** AI/ML searches large datasets for new drugs or repurposes existing drugs for new applications. Many companies use Deep Learning (DL) techniques to accurately predict how well a compound will bind to a disease target, speeding up drug discovery.
- ***Health outcomes research:*** AI/ML can analyse real-world data to determine treatment effectiveness and outcomes in different patient groups. For example, the Observational Health Data Sciences and Informatics (OHDSI) evaluate large datasets to learn about the effects of treatments in the real world.
- ***Patient Stratification:*** AI and ML analyse patient data such as health records, gene data, etc. This would mean that a person's lifestyle would be used to classify patients based on their response to treatment or specific risks. This helps in the development of personalised therapies for these diseases. For example, Flatiron Health searches patient records to identify appropriate groups for clinical trials.
- ***Safety and pharmacovigilance monitoring:*** AI and ML are used to analyse real-world data, allowing early detection of safety issues with drugs or medical devices. Systems such as IBM Watson for drug safety monitor reports for potential risks.

4.8 Decentralised Clinical Trials (DCTs)

DCTs represent one of the most recent trends in clinical research, demonstrating the potential to use digital medical devices and remote monitoring methods such as telemedicine, mobile health devices and electronic data collection and capture. This enables health records to collect patient data at home or in nearby facilities, in addition to the traditional clinical setting. Virtual consultations, wearable devices, home health visits and digital consent are all critical components. AI and ML analytics, blockchain for data security and advancements in wearable technology are some of the current DCT trends. Regulatory bodies are also becoming more supportive of DCTs, issuing guidelines to protect the integrity of data and participants. DCT offers a variety of benefits, including increased access to participants in rural or disadvantaged areas, ease of participation, which can lead to better retention and onsite management and travel cost savings. DCTs also allow faster recruitment and better data collection through continuous monitoring.

However, challenges include ensuring the technology access and literacy, maintaining data security, complying with various regulations and engaging participants remotely. The COVID-19 pandemic has accelerated the adoption of DCTs, highlighting their potential, especially in studying rare diseases. Some examples of DCTs with digital health technologies are:

- Novartis is expanding its collaboration with Science 37 to enhance its virtual clinical trials initiative. These DCTs utilise digital tools that allow patients to participate from home or at local medical facilities instead of centralised sites like hospitals. Novartis has launched the DCTs in the United States (US), focusing on dermatology, neuroscience and oncology. Leveraging Science 37's NORA® technology, patients can study via mobile devices and telemedicine. The partnership aims to integrate Science 37's tailored software into Novartis' major clinical development projects.
- ConcertAI, a part of SymphonyAI Group, is at the forefront of technology in Definitive Real-World Data (RWD) and AI solutions tailored for Precision Oncology. SymphonyAI Group is recognised as the fastest-growing collective of AI companies. ConcertAI announced an expansion of its collaboration with Pfizer Oncology in Precision Oncology. This expansion aims to utilise ConcertAI's meticulously designed Real-World Data for various clinical development endeavours across breast, lung, prostate and renal cell carcinoma cancers, fostering innovative study designs and non-interventional studies.
- Medidata has a Patient Cloud App for electronic Clinical Outcome Assessment (COA) for simplifying clinical trials by combining electronic patient-reported Outcomes (ePRO), Clinician-reported Outcomes (ClinROs) and site mode into one App. Patient Cloud App enhances workflows and patient engagement for patients, researchers and healthcare professionals. Patient Cloud App focuses on patient-centric design, making trials easier, faster and more effective for onsite clinical trials and DCTs.

AI and ML are transforming the pharmaceutical and healthcare sectors by improving diagnosis, personalising treatments and streamlining operations. AI and ML help Health Care Professional (HCPs) to make better decisions, lower costs and enhance patient care, however data privacy and ethical concerns are the major challenges.

Proposed Questions

Long Answer Type Questions (10 Marks Each)

1. How do electronic health records contribute to clinical decision support systems powered by AI and ML and improve patient care?

2. Explain the role of AI and ML in disease surveillance and outbreak detection with suitable examples in real-world scenarios.
3. Describe the significance of AI and ML in the clinical evaluation of drugs, devices and software.
4. Explain the concept of real-world evidence and its importance in patient data analysis using AI and ML in clinical development.
5. What are the current trends and future directions of AI and ML in healthcare and how do you foresee these technologies shaping the future of medicine and patient care?

Short Answer Type Questions (5 Marks Each)

1. Describe the role of AI and ML in medical diagnosis.
2. Enumerate the AI applications in disease surveillance.
3. Discuss the AI and ML algorithms to optimise resource allocation and capacity planning.
4. Discuss briefly how machine learning algorithms aid in predicting the progression of diseases.
5. Explore future possibilities for AI-enabled advancements in clinical research and evaluation.
6. How do AI and ML algorithms contribute to the early detection and monitoring of disease outbreaks?
7. What are electronic health records (EHRs)? Discuss the significance of ethics in modern healthcare.
8. What are the limitations of AI and ML in disease surveillance and outbreak detection?

Very Short Questions (1 Mark)

1. Define disease surveillance and outbreak detection.
2. Define electronic health records (EHRs).
3. Define real-world evidence in healthcare.
4. Define resource allocation and capacity planning in healthcare.
5. What are the applications of AI and ML in improving clinical trial outcomes?
6. Discuss the role of AI and ML in predicting the progression of diseases.
7. Give a note on AI and ML algorithms aiding in the early detection of disease outbreaks.

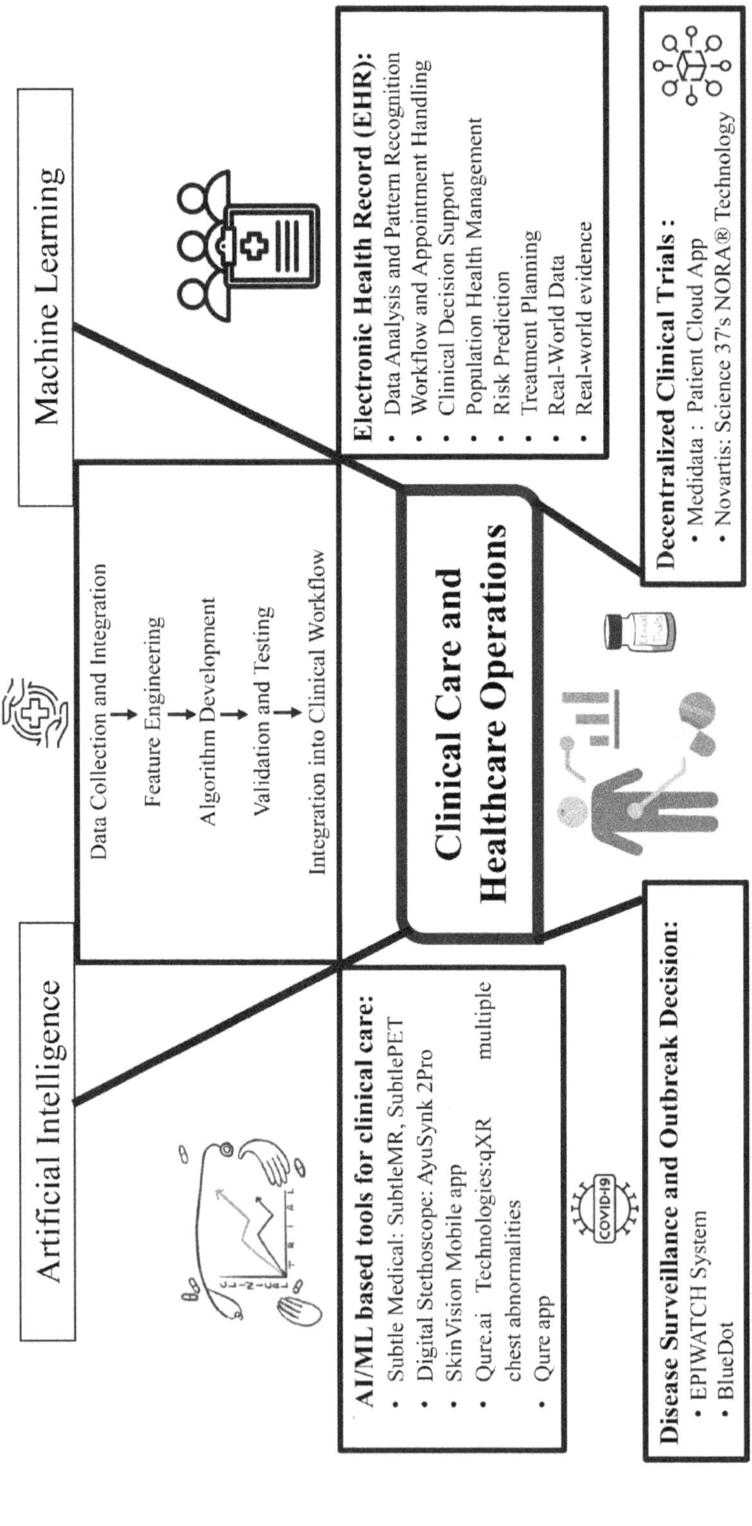

Artificial Intelligence
Machine Learning
Data Collection and Integration
Feature Engineering
Algorithm Development
Validation and Testing
Integration into Clinical Workflow
Clinical Care and Healthcare Operations
AI/ML based tools for clinical care:
• Subtle Medical: SubtleMR, SubtlePET
• Digital Stethoscope: AyuSynk 2Pro
• SkinVision Mobile app
• Qure.ai Technologies:qXR multiple chest abnormalities
• Qure app
Electronic Health Record (EHR):
• Data Analysis and Pattern Recognition
• Workflow and Appointment Handling
• Clinical Decision Support
• Population Health Management
• Risk Prediction
• Treatment Planning
• Real-World Data
• Real-world evidence
Disease Surveillance and Outbreak Decision:
• EPIWATCH System
• BlueDot
Decentralized Clinical Trials :
• Medidata : Patient Cloud App
• Novartis: Science 37's NORA® Technology
COVID-19

CHAPTER 5

Future of AI and ML in Pharmaceutical Sciences and Healthcare

5.1 Introduction

The Artificial Intelligence (AI) and Machine Learning (ML) are rapidly expanding at large extent to improve all aspects of Quality of Life (QoL). All businesses, no matter their size or nature, are using the technology of AI and ML. For example, AI and ML have significantly advanced in the healthcare sector, especially in the pharmaceutical, retail, e-commerce and manufacturing industries. Big data and predictive analytics are two basic applications of AI and ML, which have augmented the pharmaceutical industry. Critical problems faced by the pharmaceutical sector, such as quality control, are being easily solved with the help of AI-powered systems. There is a need for creative application(s) of this technology to boost production and deliver better results. Undoubtedly, AI/ML offers a considerable value proposition to the pharmaceutical industry to create new business models. The use of AI in pharmaceuticals is evident in supply chain management, marketing, drug development and manufacturing. The application of AI in the pharmaceutical industry has many advantages. For example, it reduces operating expenses for businesses, helps increase productivity in the work done by an organisation and speeds up the approval process for new drugs. This indicates excellent potential of AI and ML for drug discovery and development efforts. AI and ML in pharmaceutical sciences and healthcare have the potential to transform everything from patient care to drug discovery. These technologies can enhance healthcare by making it more efficient, effective and personalised, which ultimately benefits millions of people.

5.2 Pharmaceutical Industry 4.0

Industry 4.0, known as the Fourth Industrial Revolution, originated in 2011 at the Hannover Fair. Initially, it was introduced as the German government's technology strategy, which brought scientific and risk-based methods to manufacturing and process intelligence. The term "Industry 4.0" signifies a new era in the Industrial Revolution (IR), involving the utilisation of cyber-physical system (CPS) technology within manufacturing as illustrated in Figure 5.1.

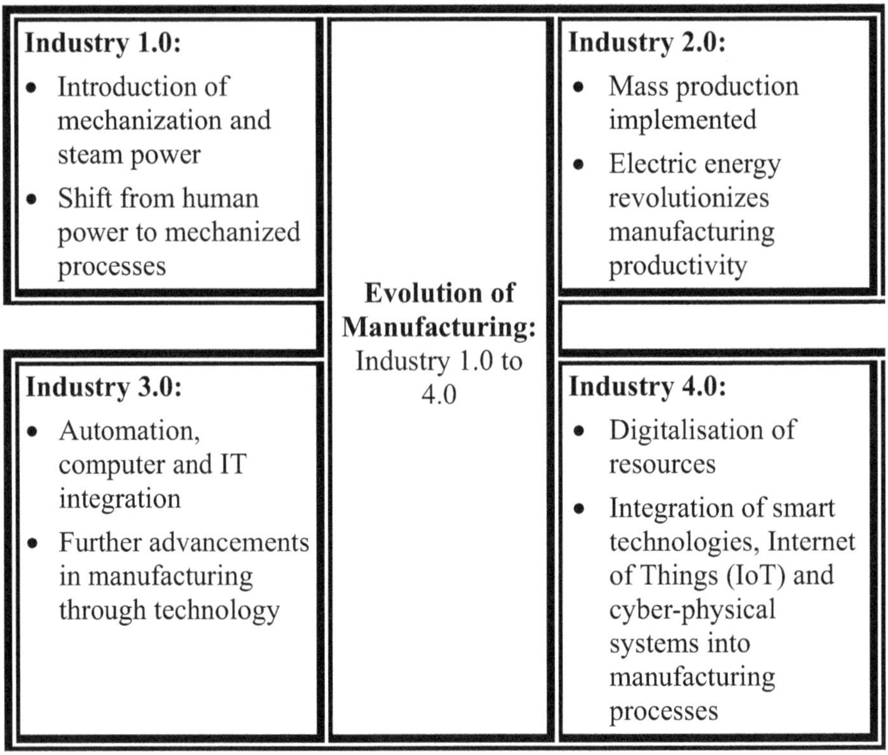

Figure 5.1 Evolution of Manufacturing: Industry 1.0 to 4.0.

This approach enhances system intelligence through interconnectivity, automation, machine learning and real-time monitoring. A special interest group within the International Society for Pharmaceutical Engineering (ISPE) has now labelled this concept as Pharma 4.0.

The Pharma 4.0 emphasises the significance of data and manufacturing intelligence. These principles include the digitalisation of resources, workforce evolution, organisational and process optimisation and a holistic control strategy. The focus is on life cycle management, culture, communication, decision-making, information systems and holistic value network integration with traceability. The design also prioritises the data integrity. The key elements of Pharma 4.0 are presented in Table 5.1.

Table 5.1 Key elements of Pharma 4.0.

S.No.	Key Element	Requirement
1.	Resources	Various components needed for Pharma 4.0 implementation, including technology, infrastructure and people.
2.	Digitalization	Core principle of Pharma 4.0, encompassing the use of digital technologies throughout the pharmaceutical value chain.
3.	Workforce	Need for a skilled and adaptable workforce equipped to handle the digital transformation in the pharmaceutical industry.
4.	Accessible	Availability of knowledgeable individuals to utilize Pharma 4.0 processes and equipment for better outcomes.
5.	Holistic Control Strategy	Approach for Quality Control (QC) based on automation and data analysis enables continuous observation to understand what happens at any given time. It helps decision-makers to finalize the well-informed choices.
6.	Life Cycle Management	Life cycle, including development, manufacturing and distribution of a product is managed digitally.
7.	Organization and processes	Need for organisational processes and structures that promote digitalisation.
8.	Culture	Need for a culture to facilitate the implementation of Pharma 4.0 that values change, collaboration and continuous learning.
9.	Communication	Efficient communication at all organisational levels to guarantee that everyone is very well aware of digital transformation.
10.	Decision Making	Data and insights from Pharma 4.0 technologies are utilized to make informed decisions.
11.	Overall Network Integration and Traceability	Need for transparent and seamless integration across the pharmaceutical value chain (from distributors to suppliers).
12.	Information systems	Information Technology (IT) frameworks that supports Pharma 4.0 and empowers data collection, collaboration and analysis.
13.	Data Integrity by Design	Building data integrity into systems and processes to ensure compliance and reliability from the outset.

In the pharmaceutical sector, the application of Cyber Physical System (CPS) in drug production can revolutionize biotechnology and pharmaceutical company control and management systems, commonly referred to as the Pharma 4.0 revolution. Pharma 4.0 encompasses various transformative changes, including implementing high-confidence medical devices and systems, advancements in drug design and development, on-demand drug production, the emergence of 3D-printed drug products, Logistic 4.0 for drug distribution management and adopting green waste management practices. It essentially represents the manifestation of Industry 4.0 principles in the pharmaceutical industry, characterised by the integration of Medical Cyber-Physical Systems (MCPS) at different stages of the drug development life cycle. MCPS, defined as life-critical, context-aware, networked systems comprising medical tools and devices, actively contribute to patient treatment protocols. The primary objectives of incorporating this paradigm in the drug development process are to reduce developmental costs and cycle time, while simultaneously enhancing the quality of drug products. This is achieved by improving the intelligence of contributors (including humans, tools and devices) and connecting & integrating these smart contributors. This system will provide awareness information and real-time status to regulatory authorities and other stakeholders as well.

The technology of cyber-physical systems (CPSs) is leveraged by the MCPSs to deliver high- continuous care for patients in complex medical scenarios (e. g. clinical trials). Cyber Physical Systems represent the integrations of networking and computation with physical processes. The embedded computers and networks monitor and control physical processes through feedback loops.

The Pharma 4.0, involving six stages (for digital maturity) is shown in Figure 5.2. The initial step involves computerization, automating manual processes, followed by connectivity, where production equipment is linked to networks for data exchange. Subsequent stages include visibility, transparency, predictability, adaptability and culminating in real-time adjustments through continuous data collection and advanced analytics.

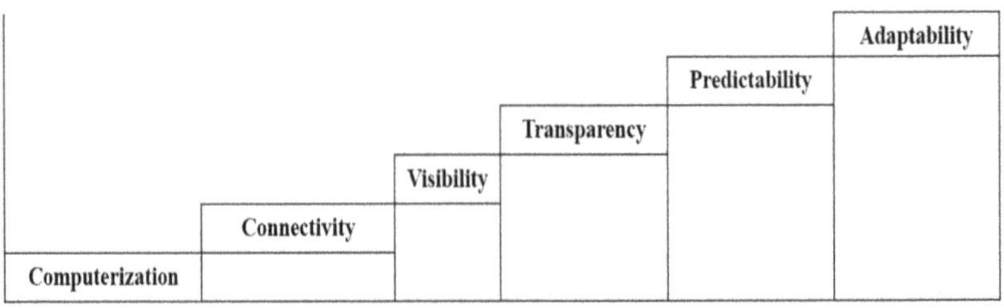

Figure 5.2 Stages of Pharma 4.0.

Practical applications of Pharma 4.0 include electronic logbooks for streamlined data documentation, digital line clearance to simplify processes and electronic batch records for continuous data collection and validation. Process visibility is enhanced through IoT devices and human-centric applications, enabling a detailed assessment of worker performance. Additionally, applications (Apps) for manufacturing technology offer pharmaceutical-specific training programs that provide specialized methods for onboarding skilled workers. Some practical applications related to the pharmaceutical sector which are already making a difference are:

Streamlining the process and enhancing data integrity:

- Electronic logbooks: Data capture automation replaces paper records, ensuring accuracy and traceability.
- Line Clearance: Digitalize cleaning processes to minimise downtime and reduce the risk of contamination.
- Electronic Batch Records: These will digitise documents for ease of review and analysis and increase quality control over all the data.

Personalised medicine and targeted therapy:

- AI-powered drug discovery: It has the potential to accelerate the process of finding new therapeutic targets and creating customised regimens.
- 3D Printing of Pharmaceuticals: It is being utilized to design personalised medicines with precise dosage and release profiles.
- Big Data Analytics: It analyse all the data (from patient information to the size of entire population groups) to predict individual drug responses and enable tailgating.

Encouraging agility and efficiency in manufacturing:

- Smart factories: The smart factories enabled with new industrial revolution will increase the flexibility and responsiveness by automating tasks with robots and other intelligent systems.
- Process visibility: Data analysis and real-time monitoring provide insights to maximise output, cut waste and guarantee quality.
- Continuous manufacturing: It eliminates batch-based production to reduce costs and turnaround time.

Other Applications:

- Digital Twins: It is used to test and optimise manufacturing processes and run a virtual model of them.
- Blockchain technology: It will help to combat counterfeit medicines and improve supply chain transparency.

- Augmented reality training: It will provide technicians with thorough instructions to work safer and more effectively.

Pharma 4.0 is set to revolutionize the pharmaceutical sector by providing hassle-free opportunities to boost productivity, quality and compliance. It is clear that manufacturers who successfully integrate digital transformation with advanced technology like AI and ML will foster positive relationships, increase their efficiency and achieve greater flexibility, all critical elements that will contribute to their success in this new healthcare sector to a great extent. The current pharmaceutical industry is now moving towards Pharma 4.0.

5.3 Digital Health Initiatives (DHIs) and Pharmaceutical Regulatory Environment

The information and communication tools to improve patient outcomes and the overall effectiveness of the health care system using the digital technology are referred to as Digital Health Initiatives (DHIs). These initiatives leverage various technologies, such as mobile apps, wearable devices, telemedicine, Electronic Health Records (EHRs) and data analytics, to enhance healthcare services and promote better health. Digital health initiatives encompass a wide range of applications, including:

- Telemedicine is using telecommunications technology, such as video calls, phone calls and secure messaging, to provide medical services and healthcare remotely. It enables healthcare professionals to connect with patients, diagnose medical conditions, offer consultations and even deliver treatment without needing in-person visits.
- Health apps, or health applications are mobile or digital softwares designed to promote well-being, offer information and help the users to manage various aspects of their health. They include fitness trackers for activity monitoring, nutrition apps for dietary management, mental health apps for stress reduction, sleep trackers for analyzing sleep patterns and medication reminders. Some apps allow users to maintain digital health records, track specific metrics, provide support during pregnancy and parenthood, offer preliminary symptom assessments and connect users with healthcare professionals for virtual consultations. However, these apps are not substitutes for professional medical advice.
- Wearable devices are small electronic gadgets worn on the body, often as accessories or clothing. They use sensors and technology to collect health and activity data. Popular for real-time information and promoting a healthier lifestyle, these devices track physical activity, steps, distance and calories. Smartwatches offer additional features like notifications, calls and health monitoring. Fitness bands focus on activity levels, sleep and heart rate. Wearable health monitors track

specific metrics for continuous health monitoring. Sleep trackers analyze sleep patterns and suggest improvements. Fashion and lifestyle wearables combine technology with style. GPS trackers monitor routes and pace and wearable devices are integrated into workplace wellness programs for the employee health.

- Electronic Health Records (EHRs) are digital patient records storing comprehensive health information. The key features include secure storage, facilitating information exchange among healthcare providers, accessible from various locations, incorporating clinical decision support, supporting patient engagement through portals, streamlining administrative tasks for increased efficiency, enabling data analytics for trend analysis, ensuring regulatory compliance and minimizing errors associated with illegible handwriting. EHRs enhance healthcare by providing a centralized, secure and accessible platform for recording, retrieving and managing patient data.
- Health analytics uses data analysis to improve healthcare by deriving insights from large datasets, including electronic health records and patient information. It employs predictive analytics to forecast trends and risks, supporting preventive measures and personalized care. Health analytics aids in population health management, helping the organizations to target interventions and enhance overall health outcomes. It provides clinical decision support tools for evidence-based recommendations at the point of care. Additionally, it contributes to quality improvement, cost management, risk stratification, patient engagement, real-time monitoring and innovation in the healthcare industry.
- Remote Patient Monitoring (RPM) digitally collects and sends patient health data remotely. Wearable technology allows continuous monitoring, making it practical to keep track of vital indicators in real time. More importantly, it efficiently manages chronic diseases because it provides early intervention and therapy modifications. When combined with tele-health systems, RPM will empower virtual consultations for individuals and will provide access to their health information. The application of RPM, the hospital readmission rates have decreased. Health Information Exchanges (HIEs) are the technologies, which make it easier for different healthcare providers to securely share patient data, thereby improving care coordination and patient outcomes.
- Digital Therapeutics (DTx) is a family of healthcare interventions known as "DTx", which uses software to offer evidence-based medical treatments to manage, treat, or prevent diseases or conditions. These digitally mediated treatments complement and sometimes replace

traditional medical treatments, especially for behavioural and psychologically associated diseases or disorders. DTx stands out from other wellness and health products because of its thorough clinical evaluation, demonstrating its safety and effectiveness.

Over the past few years, Digital Health Technologies (DHT) have advanced the healthcare system. This involves revolutionizing the healthcare industry by using technological advancements such as AI, ML, DL and mobile medical applications. Digital health initiatives and pharmaceuticals are essential components. The regulatory environment plays a vital role in the healthcare system and is closely related to safety, efficacy, quality security and privacy. Security and privacy are two new components that regulatory authorities need to focus for the purpose to provide better outcomes in digital healthcare innovation. The interconnection between digital health initiatives and the pharmaceutical regulatory environment are:

- **Clinical trials and data management:** Clinical trials are essential for testing new drugs. Wearable technology and Electronic Health Records (EHRs) are two examples of digital health technologies that greatly simplify test data collection. Regulatory bodies are supporting innovative technology during testing as long as it follows regulatory requirements strictly.
- **Data security and privacy:** The processing of sensitive health data is also a part of digital health activities. The General Data Protection Regulation (in Europe) and Health Insurance Portability and Accountability Act (HIPAA) (in USA) regulate the data issues. To maintain data security and patient privacy, pharmaceutical businesses engaged in digital health must adhere to these standards.
- **Real-world Evidence (RWE):** Digital health generates real-world evidence, offering insights into pharmaceutical product effectiveness in daily clinical practice. The regulators recognize the value of RWE. The collaboration between digital health stakeholders and regulatory agencies is crucial to establish standards for data collection.
- **Telemedicine and Remote Patient Monitoring:** Telemedicine and remote monitoring, driven by digital health, have become prominent, especially during and after the COVID-19 pandemic. Regulatory frameworks need adaptation to ensure quality and safety standards in these new healthcare delivery modes.
- **Regulatory Compliance for Health Apps and Software:** Many digital health initiatives involve developing the medical apps and software. Regulatory agencies have specific guidelines for their approval. Pharmaceutical companies entering the digital health space must navigate these regulations for product approval.

- **Interoperability Standards:** Digital health involves multiple stakeholders. The interoperability standards are crucial for seamless data exchange. The regulatory agencies are setting interoperability and data sharing standards among healthcare providers, pharmaceutical companies and technology developers as well.

The alignment, adaptation and collaboration between digital health initiatives and pharmaceutical regulatory environment are the need of the hour. The healthcare sector should utilize these technological benefits without jeopardizing patient safety, data security, along with regulatory compliance.

5.4 World Health Organization (WHO): Ethics and Governance of Artificial Intelligence for Health

The WHO report maintains significant ethical considerations related to the use of AI in the healthcare sector. These principles are envisioned as a basis for governments, technology developers, companies, civil society and intergovernmental organizations to adopt ethical practices in responsible use of AI for better healthcare outcomes. Six basic principles of WHO related to AI are shown in Figure 5.3.

Protecting Human Autonomy	Promoting Human Well-Being and Safety and the Public Interest	Ensuring transparency, explainability and intelligibility
	WHO: Principles to ensure AI works for the public interest	
Fostering Responsibility and Accountability	Ensuring Inclusiveness and Equity	Promoting responsive and sustainable AI

Figure 5.3 WHO Principles to Ensure AI Works for the Public Interest.

- **Protecting human autonomy:** The principle of autonomy is maintained by AI while being integrated into decision-making processes. The relevant information is provided to Healthcare Professionals (HCPs) for the safe use of AI systems. AI increases the people's understanding for securing valid informed consent through legal frameworks on protecting privacy, confidentiality and data protection.
- **Promoting human well-being, safety and the public Interest:** The uses of AI guarantee the patient safety and are in compliance with all

applicable safety, accuracy and efficacy regulations. The AI applications also consider the quality control of the product. In addition, AI considers the prevention from mental or physical damage by means of alternative practices or approaches.

- **Promoting responsive and sustainable AI:** All the developers, medical professionals, patients/users, pharmacy professionals and regulators must understand the AI technology. Simply, improving the accessibility includes improving transparency and adequate pre-deployment documentation that can inform meaningful public consultation. The AI technologies must be explained very well in accordance with recipient's understanding.
- **Fostering Responsibility and Accountability:** The work must be performed correctly and have skilled employees along with equitable use conditions. All the stakeholders are accountable for perfect functioning. The accountability is also established through evaluations by patients and healthcare professionals, which may lead to 'human warranty'. Any human over sighted point may be followed by regulatory criteria. It is imperative that a redressal mechanism should be established for an individual or a community, if they suffer negative consequences from algorithmic choices.
- **Ensuring transparency, explainability and intelligibility:** The intelligent system of AI must have the fair access regardless of socio-economic or demographic characteristics. The technology should be shared widely to meet the different needs and capabilities of high-income and low-to-middle-income environments. The AI technology should be easily explainable and can be designed in a way to the level of understanding of intended audience.
- **Ensuring Inclusiveness and Equity:** The increased access of AI technology includes increased openness and provides adequate pre-deployment documentation. This document can serve as a guide to have valuable public outreach.

5.5 Digital Health vs. e-Health

The practice and delivery of healthcare is being transformed by the use of digital technologies. The concept of e-health, involving the use of computers, the Internet and mobile devices, has become crucial for improving health and healthcare services. The digital system is working alongside traditional methods in order to provide information to both patients and healthcare consumers. The emergence of e-health is desired to better document and track patients' health and procedures, mainly for insurance purposes. The advanced technology of AI has made electronic tracking system more prevalent in comparison to traditional paper records. This led to the development of telemedicine, where telecommunication technologies are used to provide healthcare remotely. Various digital tools are utilised in e-health, such as the Internet for communication with healthcare professionals, interactive TV for real-time audio-visual exchanges, kiosks for interactive information and mobile devices for instant access to health information. Despite the benefits of the advanced technology, the challenges includes the initial learning curve for adopting new technologies, financial barriers and concerns about standards and privacy.

The benefits of e-health include the reduction of the risk of adverse drug events through computerized systems. It also increases the preventive interventions through automated reminders. Consumers are benefitted by ordering online prescriptions, online access to hospital services and facilitates communication between patients and healthcare providers through text, audio, or video conferencing. The barriers to e-health adoption include financial incentives, reimbursement challenges of costs, standards and privacy. The digital divide, (a gap in access to digital technologies) is also a significant barrier, impacting those who lack access or knowledge about technology. The e-health and digital health are often used interchangeably; however there are subtle differences between these two terms, which are tabulated in Table 5.2.

Table 5.2 Differences Between e-Health and Digital Health.

Feature	e-Health	Digital Health
Focus	Supports existing healthcare system through electronic tools	Supports existing healthcare system through electronic tools including e-Health (Digital health expands the concept of e-Health)
Scope	Narrower, primarily deals with electronic information exchange and tools like EHRs	Broader, encompasses diverse digital technologies like wearables, apps and many more
Applications	Electronic health records, telemedicine, patient portals, health information networks	Wearable devices, health and fitness apps, telehealth, remote monitoring, big data analytics, AI-powered diagnostics
Target users	Primarily healthcare professionals and institutions	Patients, consumers, healthcare professionals and researchers
Benefits	Improved efficiency, better communication, easier access to information	Personalized care, preventive measures, data-driven insights, empowered patients

Table 5.2 *Contd...*

Feature	e-Health	Digital Health
Challenges	Data security, interoperability, privacy concerns, adoption by healthcare professionals	Data security, privacy concerns, digital divide, ethical considerations
Regulation	More established regulations due to focus on medical data	Evolving regulations due to rapid innovation and broader scope
Funding	Primarily from government and healthcare institutions	Diverse sources, including venture capital, grants, individual consumer spending
Future growth	Steady growth as healthcare adopts more electronic tools	Exponential growth driven by rapid evolution of digital technologies
Overall	Subset of digital health, focused on electronic solutions within healthcare system	Umbrella term encompassing all digital technologies impacting health and healthcare

Digital health broadens the idea of e-health by involving consumers' digital friendly smart, devices. It also includes the use of digital technologies like the Internet of Things, advanced computing, big data analytics, artificial intelligence (including machine learning) and robotics for health-related purposes.

5.6 e-Prescription

e-Prescription also known as electronic prescription, involves the use of digital methods to create and send prescriptions between healthcare providers and pharmacies. Instead of paper, healthcare professionals utilise specialised software for generating digital prescriptions, which often connects with Electronic Health Records (EHR) systems to access patient information seamlessly. The main components of e-prescription systems include:

- **Electronic Prescribing Software:** The particular software is used by healthcare professionals to create digital prescriptions. The integration of software with EHR systems can be made for easy access to patient information.
- **Prescription Transmission:** The prescription is sent electronically to the pharmacy's computer system, once it has been granted. The real time transmission helps to improve efficiency and accuracy.
- **Pharmacy System Integration:** The software helps to receive and process electronic prescriptions. These e-prescriptions are integrated with their dispensing and inventory management systems.

- **Patient Identification:** The accurate patient identification, reduction in errors and assurance of dispensing of proper medication are the basic feature of e-prescription.
- **Drug Interaction Checking:** The potential drug interactions, allergies, other safety considerations are checked using e-prescription software, which also helps in preventing interactions.
- **Electronic Record Keeping:** A comprehensive and accessible patient record is provided by storing the e-prescriptions electronically. The continuity of care and coordination among healthcare professionals are augmented by electronic record keeping and analysis.

Benefits of e-Prescription include:

- **Reduced Errors:** The errors associated with handwritten prescriptions can be decreased by digital prescriptions.
- **Improved Efficiency:** The digital prescription process is streamlined resulting in faster and more efficient information for pharmacies and health care professionals.
- **Enhanced Medication Adherence:** The electronic prescriptions are easily shared and refilled, thereby benefit the patients towards improved adherence and medication regimens.
- **Better Communication:** The communication between healthcare professionals, patients and pharmacies, is improved by e-prescription leading to smooth coordination of care.
- **Reduced scams:** The chances of prescription scams can be reduced due to inbuilt security feature in electronic prescription.

The patient care quality is being enhanced by the adoption of e-prescription throughout the world. The interoperability, data security & regulatory concerns are the challenges towards full fledge adoption by healthcare providers and pharmacies.

5.7 Telemedicine

The term telemedicine consists of two words "*tele*," meaning "*distance*" and word "*medicine,*" meaning "t*o heal*". The combination of communication technology and e-information is used by health care professionals for providing services to a distant patient/participant. According to the World Health Organization (WHO), "*The delivery of healthcare services by all healthcare professionals using information and communication technologies for the exchange of valid information for diagnosis, treatment and prevention of disease and injuries, research and evaluation and for the continuing education of healthcare providers, all in the interests of advancing the health of individuals and their communities.*"

Telemedicine offer the healthcare services remotely by the application of telecommunications. The video conferencing for real-time consultations, telehealth platforms for virtual appointments, remote monitoring using wearable devices, asynchronous communication through messaging or secure portals and digital imaging for diagnostic analysis are the different segments of telemedicine. The telehealth platform utilizes the integration of AI by incorporating ML algorithms and data analytics. The processes like data analysis, image recognition, natural language processing and virtual consultations are streamlined by integration of AI with telemedicine. The improved accessibility, enhanced diagnoses, personalized treatment plans and efficient remote patient monitoring are the various benefits of AI in telemedicine.

The engagements of chatbots with patients for preliminary assessments of symptoms and offering round-the-clock support are playing a vital role in telemedicine. The ethical and privacy concerns (related to data security), patient consent and algorithm bias are the major challenges in adopting AI in healthcare. The applications like telepsychiatry for mental healthcare, predictive analytics and remote monitoring devices, are the latest developments provided by AI in telemedicines.

ICU Digital Powered-AI: ICU

CLEW Virtual ICU is a cutting-edge AI-driven platform, which has revolutionized the healthcare system. This system has augmented the decision-making efficiency. The patient care has been optimized by streamlining workflows, improving communication and implementing care effectively using this technology. It identifies and intervenes early, prioritizing patient context and increasing case volumes. CLEW ICU works with current Electronic Medical Records (EMR) and Medical Devices (MDs), either on-site or in the cloud. The ML is also utilized to review detailed medical records and generate a personalized risk score, helping doctors to spot high-risk patients and avoid complications. The main features are:

- Real-time monitoring of patient data
- Alerts for potential complications
- Clinical decision support tools
- Communication tools for collaborative care

CLEW ICU, with its powerful technology, not only improves clinical outcomes but also delivers cost-effective and efficient care, ultimately enhancing the overall experience for providers, patients and their families.

AI-driven virtual reality in telemedicine reshapes medical training, patient education and therapy, offering mesmerizing experiences for medical practitioners. AI-based decision support systems empower healthcare providers with relevant patient data and clinical guidelines for more precise diagnoses and personalized care plans. The healthcare professionals can share knowledge and best practices globally leading to foster innovation by collaborative AI network models. The needs of aging populations and individuals with chronic conditions, facilitating remote monitoring, medication reminders and timely interventions are being addressed easily with AI/ML technology.

5.8 Digital Health Intervention (DHI)

A Digital Health Intervention (DHI) is a specific technological tool to support health and related fields. It is created to tackle a particular problem of healthcare system to achieve a defined goal. The AI/ML algorithms, wearable devices, mobile health apps, telemedicine services and other digital tools are well known examples. The WHO is recommending the countries to use smartphones, health technology, wearables, telemedicine and personalised medicine for advancing sustainable health development and achieving universal health coverage. The health information and support have become more accessible and effective by the use of digital tools. These interventions are classified by World Health Organization (WHO) to provide a framework for understanding to improve healthcare. The DHIs classification is shown in Figure 5.4.

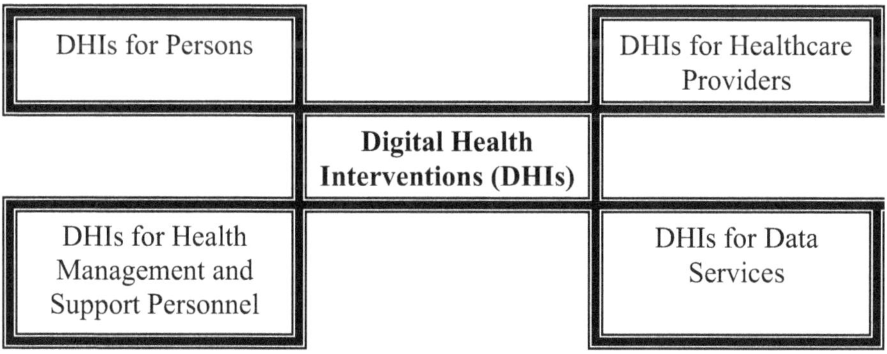

Figure 5.4 Classification of Digital Health Interventions.

5.8.1 Digital Health Interventions for Persons

Digital Health Interventions (DHIs) for persons encompass a wide range of technologies and applications designed to improve health and well-being of the patients. The subsets with impact are:

Targeted Communication to Persons:

- ***Transmit Health Event Alerts to Specific Population Group(s):*** The notifications about health events are transferred like disease outbreaks to specific populations. Example: In Uganda, Short Message Service (SMS) alerts were used during an Ebola outbreak, CoWIN app during COVID-19 in India.

- ***Transmit Targeted Health Information to Persons:*** The customized communication provides health education and promotion based on an individual's health or demographic information. Example: A mobile system providing information regarding pregnancy to pregnant women.
- ***Transmit Targeted Alerts and Reminders to Persons:*** The reminders and alerts are sent for preventive services, appointments and medication adherence. Example: An app sending SMS reminders for upcoming mother and child health services.
- ***Transmit Diagnostics Results or Availability to Persons***: The laboratory results are shared with individuals, such as HIV test results. Example: An app delivering CD4 count results to patients tested for HIV.

Untargeted Communication to Persons:

- ***Transmit Untargeted Health Information to an Undefined Population:*** The mass communication campaigns delivering identical health messages to a broad audience. Example: Launching SMS messages to inform the community about maternal and neonatal health services.
- ***Transmit Untargeted Health Event Alerts to an Undefined Group:*** Sending untargeted alerts about public health events to a general audience. Example: Senegal's Ministry of Health sends SMS messages to raise awareness about Ebola.

Person to Person Communication:

- ***Peer Group for Individuals:*** Facilitating communication between individuals as peers within organized networks or groups. Example: Peer-led support groups for HIV-infected adolescents.

Personal Health Tracking:

- ***Access by the Individual to Own Medical or Summary Health Records:*** Allow the individuals to access and track their health records. Example: Electronic personal health records augmenting medical records with self-gathered health data.
- ***Self-monitoring of Health or Diagnostic Data by the Individual:*** Using wearables and sensors for personal health monitoring. Example: Applications tracking activity, exercise, food, weight and sleep.
- ***Active Data Capture/Documentation by an Individual:*** Individuals documenting health status and activities. Example: A period-tracking

application helping women to monitor the fertility issues and other challenges.

- ***Access by the Individual to Verifiable Documentation of a Health Event or Status:*** Providing individuals with access to verifiable credentials confirming their health status. Example: Applications offering certificates for insurance or vaccination status.

Person Based Reporting:

- ***Reporting of Health System Feedback by Persons***: Allowing individuals to provide feedback on health system issues. Example: A text-based youth engagement tool enabling reporting on community issues.
- ***Reporting of Public Health Events by Persons***: Individuals reporting on public health events, such as disease outbreaks, through platforms like SMS. Example: Citizens reporting suspected Ebola cases via SMS.

On-Demand Communication with Persons:

- ***Look-up of Information on Health and Health Services by Individuals:*** Individuals searching for health information, services, or scheduling appointments. Example: An online source providing clear health information accessible via computer or mobile device.
- ***Simulated Human-like Conversations with Individuals:*** Interactive conversations with individuals through chatbots or AI. Example: Chatbots generate quality responses to patient questions in an online forum.

Person-Centered Financial Transactions:

- ***Transmit or Manage Out-of-Pocket Payments by Individuals***: Facilitating mobile money payments for health services directly made by individuals. Example: A maternal health smart card allowing prepaid access to specific services.
- ***Transmit or Manage Vouchers to Individuals for Health Services:*** Issuing and redeeming health vouchers through mobile finance. Example: SMS money transfers reimbursing social franchise service providers for family planning services.
- ***Transmit or Manage Incentives to Individuals for Health Services***: Providing cash transfers to individuals based on health-related behaviours. Example: A vaccine registry system using SMS reminders and cash transfers to encourage vaccination.

Person-Centered Consent Management:

- ***Manage Provision and Withdrawal of Consent by Individuals:*** Digital tools managing the process of providing, reviewing and withdrawing consent for personal information and health records. Example: Apps that help to control who can use individual personal information like photos and health records, by allowing the concerned person to provide, review, or withdraw the consent easily.

5.8.2 Digital Health Interventions for Healthcare Providers (HCPs)

The classification within this group outlines the abilities of digital technology that can be used to accomplish goals aimed at helping HCPs. HCPs are professionals within the health workforce who administer health interventions. Diverse digital tools support healthcare providers in identification, record-keeping, decision support, telemedicine, communication, referral coordination, scheduling, training, prescription management, laboratory/diagnostics and financial transactions. Various functionalities in the subset aimed at improving healthcare delivery by DHI are:

Identification and Registration of Persons:

- **Verify a person's unique identity:** It utilizes biometrics, like fingerprint recognition for person's identity. Example: drug treatment and adherence tracking for tuberculosis patient.
- **Enrol person(s) for health services:** The mobile health application facilitates the registration of pregnancies at government health facilities.

Person-Centred Health Records:

- **Longitudinal tracking of person's health status and services:** It includes digitized registers for health programs, case management logs and virtual vaccination registries.

Healthcare Provider Decision Support:

- **Provide prompts and alerts based on protocol:** The tablet-based application alerts to healthcare providers based on WHO guidelines for critical observations.

Telemedicine:

- **Consultations between remote persons and healthcare providers:** The toll-free health hotline staffed by trained health workers for clinical guidance over the phone.
- **Remote monitoring of a person's health or diagnostic data by provider:** The mobile health monitoring, by using body sensor networks.

Healthcare Provider Communication:

- **Communication from healthcare provider to supervisor(s):** A two-way, mobile phone-based system connecting ministries of health and health workers via SMS.

- **Communication and performance feedback to healthcare provider(s):** A mobile health platform provides detailed performance feedback through weekly calls.

Referral Coordination:

- **Coordinate emergency response and transport:** A mobile phone with a decision support application ensures that health facilities are prepared for emergencies.

Scheduling and Activity Planning for Healthcare Providers:

- **Identify persons in need of services:** A digital platform integrates scheduling and service reminder tools.

Healthcare Provider Training:

- **Provide training content to healthcare provider(s):** A mobile platform delivers training to health workers through video instruction and reference materials.

Prescription and Medication Management:

- **Transmit or track prescription orders:** The pharmacy management applications facilitate prescription order tracking.

Laboratory and Diagnostics Imaging Management

- **Transmit a person's diagnostic result to a healthcare provider:** An SMS system alerts to clinic workers for prepared test (clinical and non-clinical) results.

Healthcare Provider Financial Transactions

- **Verify individual's health coverage and financing scheme membership:** An online eligibility check-in allows verification of beneficiaries.

5.8.3 Digital Health Interventions for Health Management and Support Personnel (HMSP)

Health Management and Support Personnel (HMSP) play a crucial role in overseeing health systems. Their responsibilities include managing the supply chain, overseeing financial aspects and handling human resources. Interventions in this category focus on utilizing digital technology to enhance capabilities and achieve objectives in health system administration as mentioned below:

Human Resource Management:

- ***List health workforce cadres:*** The tracking, management, deployment and mapping of health workforce is facilitated by software, for example, iHRIS by IntraHealth International.

- ***Monitor performance of healthcare providers***: The mobile learning solutions for community health extension workers with weekly performance reports.
- ***Manage registration/certification of healthcare providers:*** The digital human resources information system for efficient verification of qualifications, registration and certification of health care providers.
- ***Record training credentials of healthcare providers:*** An electronic system for tracking and updating training qualifications.

Supply Chain Management:

- ***Manage inventory and distribution of health commodities:*** An electronic Logistics Management Information System (ELMIS) for monitoring of family planning commodities.
- ***Notify stock levels of health commodities:*** A SMS-based system for stockout prevention and coordination.
- ***Monitor cold-chain sensitive commodities:*** A SMS-based system with sensors for monitoring vaccine temperature conditions, etc.

Public Health Event Notification:

- ***Notification of public health events from the point of diagnosis:*** An automated SMS or email alert for detecting or Manage Detection and Response (MDR).

Civil Registration and Vital Statistics (CRVS):

- ***Notify, register and certify birth events:*** A mobile data collection for birth and death notification, facilitating the issuance of certificates.
- ***Notify, register and certify death events:*** Health workers using SMS for notifying death events.

Health System Financial Management:

- ***Register and verify health coverage scheme membership of persons:*** Mobile enrolment app for large-scale health schemes through secured digital administration.
- ***Track and manage insurance billing and claims processes:*** An e-claims system for submitting and processing health insurance claims.

Equipment and Asset Management:

- ***Monitor status and maintenance of health equipment***: The mechanisms for updating and tracking maintenance needs of physical assets in health facilities.

Facility Management:

- ***List health facilities and related information***: A master health facility list with unique IDs and locations.

Person-Centred Health Certificate Management:

- ***Register and store current health certificate information:*** A digital immunization certificate for documentation and issuance.
- ***Retrieve and validate current health certificate information, revoke and update health certificate:*** Confirming a person's status by accessing a subset of their health record.

5.8.4 Digital Health Interventions for Data Services

This involves the implementation of digital technology to support a range of activities related to data management, use and compliance with data governance. It encompasses various aspects of managing, analyzing and ensuring the integrity of health-related data. These interventions fall into several categories:

Data Management:

- ***Form Creation for Data Acquisition***: The electronic tools like OpenDataKit (an open-source suite of tools that allows data collection) for mobile-based surveys and questionnaire administration.
- ***Data Storage and Aggregation:*** Platforms like the Global Health Observatory Data Repository (GHODR) for organizing and storing health-related statistics.

Data Coding:

- ***Parse Unstructured Data:*** Developing automated algorithms for cleaning and linking unstructured information to structured datasets.
- ***Merge, Deduplicate and Curate Coded Datasets***: Managing health informatics terminology standards for standardized data.

Geospatial Information Management:

- ***Map Location of Health Facilities/Structures and Households:***Global Positioning System (GPS) mapping for health facility locations and Geographic Information Systems (GIS) mapping for tracking disease outbreaks.
- ***Map Location of Persons and Settlements***: Implementing web-based tools for mapping coverage areas and population density.

Data Exchange and Interoperability:

- ***Point-to-Point Data Integration:*** Establishing a national health information exchange platform to facilitate communication between health systems.

- ***Standards-Compliant Interoperability:*** Enabling information exchange through interoperability layers and technical standards.

Data Governance Compliance:

- ***Authentication and Authorization:*** Using digital tools for identity verification and role-based access control.
- ***Data Privacy Protection:*** Employing applications to secure and sensitive data.
- ***Data Consent and Provenance:*** Implementing consent management systems for controlling personal data collection and usage.

5.9 Digital Health Interventions - Case Studies

To make the information more relatable and applicable to real-world situations some case studies related to Digital Health Interventions (DHIs) are mentioned below:

5.9.1 U-report/UNICEF Uganda Strategy - Ebola Outbreak (August 2012)

In August 2012, Uganda grappled with a funding and resource challenge in responding to the Ebola outbreak, as reported by the Ministry of Health and WHO. In collaboration with UNICEF, U-report implemented a communication plan with three main objectives. Firstly, they disseminated crucial information through SMS alerts to Kibaale and neighbouring districts, focusing on Ebola symptoms, spread and prevention methods. A question-and-answer session was also scheduled to engage the community. Secondly, the U-report interface facilitated real-time responses to community questions and concerns, with messages prioritized based on urgency. The 72 SMS messages were addressed with 24 hours out of 1000 SMS received. The community feedback was received by conducting a poll from 15 % of U-reporters. The feedback revealed that 67% people found that information is useful. The wider communication plans, addressing community concerns and gathering valuable insights highlighted the role of U-report. This case study emphasizes the Ebola crisis can be easily managed by U-report's strategic communication and offers lessons for future strategies in case of emergency.

5.9.2 Ayushman Bharat Digital Mission (ABDM)

Ayushman Bharat Digital Mission (ABDM) is an Indian government initiative to establish a strong digital health infrastructure. The improvement of healthcare accessibility, creation of national digital health ecosystem and assurance of security of health information are the primary goals of this initiation. The various digital systems, introduced are Ayushman Bharat Health Account (ABHA) (number for unique identification), a Personal Health Record (PHR) (mobile app for individuals), a Healthcare Professionals

Registry (HPR) and a Health Facility Registry (HFR). The unique identifier is ABHA number, which allows secure linkage of health records across different systems with patient consent. The PHR mobile app is useful for the purpose of managing health information. It is useful in creating an ABHA Address, accessing the health information, linking the records and managing the consents. The Healthcare Professionals Registry (HPR) serves as a comprehensive database of all healthcare professionals. It promotes the connectivity within India's digital health ecosystem. In a similar manner, the Health Facility Registry (HFR) is a repository for both public and private health facilities. The transparency and accessibility in healthcare service delivery are the objectives of ABDM. The secure storage benefits the patients in sharing of medical records, accessing the remote health services and making informed decisions. The improved access to patient histories, facilitating more effective interventions and continuity of care are the advantages for healthcare professionals. The policymakers can gain access to data for informed decision-making and researchers can utilize the aggregated information for program evaluations as well.

5.9.3 Robotics Middleware for Healthcare (RoMi-H) in Singapore Public Health Institutions

The Robotics Middleware for Healthcare (RoMi-H) is a solution for diverse systems within Singapore Public Health Institutions (PHIs). Operating on the Robot Operating System 2 (ROS 2) framework, RoMi-H acts as a central communication layer, harmonizing medical devices, robotic systems, user interfaces, building infrastructure, IoT devices and Hospital Information Systems (HIS). The efficient infrastructure management, multi-fleet coordination through a scalable system, virtual simulation tool for optimal traffic modeling and access to a robust set of development and integration tools are the key features of ROMi-H. The Robotics, Automation and Interfaces Scheduling Engine (RAISE) complement vendor fleet managers and act as a high-level planner for robotic task assignment and execution. The traffic flows, optimization of the robotic ecosystem and resolving conflicts are being prioritized by the RAISE. The RoMi-H streamlines operations and helps to standardized security protocols, reduce technical risks and accelerate the deployment of automation solutions to meet the growing demand for advanced technology in healthcare.

5.9.4 Transforming Pneumonia Care: CAPE AI Predictive Engine

In Singapore, Changi General Hospital (CGH) and the Integrated Health Information System (IHiS) collaborated to create the Community-Acquired Pneumonia and COVID-19 Artificial Intelligence Predictive Engine (CAPE). The chest X-ray images are utilized by this tool to rapidly predict pneumonia severity, assisting healthcare professionals in efficiently allocating resources during pandemics. The major advantage of CAPE is to provide quick severity predictions, enabling clinicians to identify patients requiring in-patient or critical care support. The training by 3,000 chest X-ray images and 200,000 data points was used to develop CAPE, which generates scores indicating low-risk pneumonia, mortality risk and critical care support risk. The CGH observed an approximate 80% accuracy in predicting severe pneumonia in comparison to manual methods. CAPE has been integrated into radiology workstations as a user-friendly desktop application. The future aspect is to include more clinical data and exploring the global collaboration by offering CAPE as freeware on a research platform(s).

5.9.5 CoWIN - Revolutionizing Vaccination Through Digital Innovation in India

India's Covid Vaccine Intelligence Network, CoWIN emerged as a transformative digital health intervention (since its launch in January 2021). The focus was to streamlining the COVID-19 vaccination program throughout the nation. The purpose was to have significant impact on efficient immunization of the large portion of India's population. The main features of CoWIN's are management of registration, appointment scheduling and real-time tracking of vaccine administration. This platform has the ability to enhance accessibility, improve efficiency and promote transparency, addressing diverse demographics (multi-lingual interface) and online booking options. The collaborations and partnerships of public and private sectors facilitated the development of CoWIN and its rapid scaling. The data-driven decision-making, valuable insights on vaccine coverage and adverse effects are the major significance in public health. In future, the integration of CoWIN with other healthcare systems and its insights will showcase its potential for creating a robust digital health ecosystem for various interventions. The digital divide is crucial to ensure the equitable access to healthcare services through digital platforms. CoWIN's achievements have make it a noteworthy example in the field of digital health improvements.

5.10 Digital Data Safety

Data plays a crucial role in the process of digitalization across various industries and sectors. The phrase *'data is the new oil'* highlights the growing significance of data in the modern digitalization era. In the all sectors, data has played a pivotal role for several decades. The conventional data in the pharmaceutical field refers to the traditional sources supporting drug development, clinical trials and healthcare practices. The integration of AI and ML has revolutionized how data is utilised in drug discovery, clinical trials and patient care in more efficiently. Some of the differences between traditional data and AI/ML-associated data in the pharmaceutical industry are shown in Table 5.3.

Table 5.3 Traditional Data and AI & ML Associated Data in the Pharmaceutical Sector.

Features	Traditional Data	AI and ML Data
Data Type	Historical records, clinical trials, patient demographics	Predictive analytics, machine learning models, deep learning models, real-time monitoring
Nature of Information	Descriptive and static data	Predictive, adaptive and dynamic data
Source	Electronic Health Records (EHRs), clinical trials, patient data, post-market surveillance	Genomic data, real-world evidence, literature mining
Use Cases	Clinical trials, patient management, regulatory submissions	Drug discovery, personalized medicine, real-time monitoring, digital clinical trial/ decentralized clinical trils.
Processing Approach	Typically, manual or rule-based processes	Automated algorithms, machine learning models
Time Horizon	Historical and retrospective	Real-time and predictive
Objective	Documenting past events, compliance with regulations	Predicting outcomes, optimizing processes, improving efficiency
Examples	Electronic Health Records (EHR), clinical trial results, patient demographics	Predictive analytics for patient recruitment and drug discovery using ML models

The principles ALCOA+, which stand for Attributable, Legible, Contemporaneous, Original, Accurate and Complete (ALCOA+), emphasize the importance of traceability, clarity, timely recording, authenticity, precision and comprehensive documentation in data management. In the pharmaceutical industry, the ALCOA+ principles play a crucial role in ensuring the integrity and reliability of data throughout its lifecycle. The ALCOA+ principles are like a guide to maintaining trustworthy data in the pharmaceutical field.

The data-driven digitalization is transforming the pharmaceutical sector. The data integrity is like guaranteeing that an Individual's or organizations data or information is accurate and trustworthy. The data safety acts as a shield, protecting individuals' or organization's data from potential threats and unauthorized access. The protection of sensitive information, mitigating cybersecurity threats and maintaining the data integrity throughout the product lifecycle are the major challenges in light of the regulatory compliance in the pharmaceutical sector. Some key aspects of digital safety data in the pharmaceutical industry are:

- ***Automated Data Analysis***: The automated analysis of large volumes of data can be performed by digital tools to identify potential safety concerns. The AI and ML algorithms are being used for pattern recognition and data mining.
- ***Automated Signal Detection***: The potential safety signals are identified with the help of digital tools. These tools analyze the large datasets for patterns or trends, which may indicate previously unrecognized risks.
- ***Data Integrity and Traceability***: The integrity and traceability of data safety can be enhanced through blockchain technology by providing a secure and transparent way to record and verify transactions. The reliability of safety information is the major concern.
- ***Data Protection***: The robust cybersecurity measures need to be implemented to protect against unauthorized access, data breaches and cyber threats due to sensitive nature of data.
- ***Data Standardization***: Standardized data formats and coding systems are employed to ensure consistency and interoperability in safety data reporting and analysis.
- ***Digital Reporting Systems***: The digital platforms are adopted by pharmaceutical companies to collect and manage adverse event reports. The in-time and accurate submission of safety information is facilitated by these platform for data submission to regulatory authorities.
- ***eClinical Trial Platforms***: The monitoring and management of safety data during clinical trials is performed by digital platform. These platforms enable real-time tracking of adverse events, protocol deviations and other safety-related information.
- **Electronic Submission Standards:** Pharmaceutical companies adhere to electronic submission standards set by regulatory agencies for reporting safety data. A standardized and efficient process for sharing safety information is ensured by digital means.
- **Integration with Healthcare Systems:** The Electronic Health Records (EHRs) are controlled by big pharma companies to gather real-world data regarding the safety and efficacy of their products. Integration with healthcare systems allows the continuous monitoring of patient outcomes.

In this digital age, data safety is not just an option, but a necessity for the pharmaceutical sector. The protection of sensitive information builds trust, ensures compliance and fosters responsible innovation within the pharmaceutical industry.

5.11 Data Privacy Impact on the Pharmaceutical Sector

Data Privacy involves the safeguarding of personal and sensitive information, ensuring that data is handled appropriately. The focus is on granting individuals the right to determine when, how and to what extent their personal information is shared or disclosed. With the increase in the number of internet users, the significance of data privacy has been heightened. In the pharmaceutical industry, massive amounts of data are collected and processed for commercial purposes, raising privacy concerns among consumers. Strengths, Weaknesses, Opportunities, Threats (SWOT) analysis for the impact of data privacy on the pharmaceutical industry is shown in Figure 5.5.

Strengths:	**Weaknesses:**
o Patient Trust o Innovation Opportunities o Regulatory Compliance	o Data Breach Risks o Compliance Costs o Complexity in Global Operations
Opportunities: o Market Differentiation o Collaboration Potential o Data-Driven Decision-Making	**Threats:** o Legal and Reputational Risks o Cybersecurity Threats o Changing Regulations

Figure 5.5 SWOT analysis for the impact of data privacy on the pharmaceutical industry.

Pharmaceutical companies are gaining strength by following data privacy rules, meeting legal standards and earning the trust of regulators and customers. The patient confidence and encouragement for sharing accurate information securely are building the robust data privacy measures. The data analytics for drug discovery and personalized medicine, fostering new opportunities within the industry depends on secure data system. The data breach risks, exposing sensitive patient information and leading to legal consequences and reputational damage are the major weakness. The compliance with stringent data privacy regulations comes with high costs, straining financial resources for infrastructure and processes. The global operations also add complexity, as adhering to diverse data privacy laws across countries becomes more challenging. Pharmaceutical companies are ensuring data privacy and attracting persons having secure health information. Strong privacy measures enable collaboration and efficiency in healthcare. Improved data privacy supports better decision-making for faster drug development and innovative research.

The data privacy laws must be followed strictly to avoid any legal problems, otherwise may lead to damaged reputation of the firm. The data is much valuable and in view of constant risk of cyber attacks and changing privacy rules globally, the updation of pharmaceutical companies is must to avoid any compliance issues.

Data privacy brings both challenges and chances for the pharmaceutical industry. The collaborative effects of companies with regulatory agencies can navigate this carefully by striking a balance between using data and people's privacy rights. It is important to handle information responsibly for the benefit of everyone involved.

Proposed Questions

Long Answer Type Questions (10 Marks Each)

1. Describe the potential impact of regulatory changes on the adoption and evolution of digital health initiatives in the pharmaceutical sector.
2. Discuss the diverse applications of digital health initiatives in modern healthcare. Provide examples to illustrate how these applications contribute to improving patient care and healthcare outcomes?
3. Explain the concept of Pharmaceutical Industry 4.0. How does it integrate advanced technologies to improve the pharmaceutical sector?
4. Explain the significance of the World Health Organization's (WHO) involvement in establishing ethics and governance frameworks for Artificial Intelligence (AI) in healthcare.
5. Explain the stages of Pharma 4.0. Discuss the key technological advancements and process improvements at each stage and how they contribute to the overall transformation of the pharmaceutical industry.
6. Provide examples of successful case studies utilizing AI and ML in pharmaceutical science and healthcare.
7. What are the challenges faced by pharmaceutical companies when implementing digital health solutions?

Short Answer Type Questions (5 Marks Each)

1. Compare the traditional data with AI and ML-associated data in terms of their applicability and impact on pharmaceutical sector.
2. Define an e-Prescription and outline its scope in modern healthcare systems. Discuss its significance in improving medication management and patient safety.
3. Describe a brief overview of Digital Health Interventions (DHIs) in digital technologies to improve health outcomes.
4. Describe three key principles outlined by the World Health Organization (WHO) to ensure Artificial Intelligence (AI) works for the public interest in healthcare.

5. Discuss the importance of digital safety data in pharmaceutical research and development.
6. How does data privacy affect the operations of pharmaceutical sector?
7. How does digitalization impact traditional pharmaceutical processes and operations?
8. What are the key technologies driving the implementation of Pharma 4.0 in the pharmaceutical sector?
9. What is telemedicine and how does it affect technology to provide healthcare services remotely? Discuss the advantages of telemedicine for patients and healthcare providers.
10. What is the key difference between 'e-Health' and 'Digital Health' and how do these differences influence their respective implementations in healthcare systems?

Very Short Questions (1 Mark)

1. Define e-health and discuss its significance in modern healthcare systems.
2. Describe Telemedicine and its impact on patient care delivery.
3. Discuss the implications of data privacy regulations on pharmaceutical companies.
4. Give the role of digital health initiatives in shaping the pharmaceutical regulatory environment.
5. How are Digital Health Interventions transforming healthcare practices?
6. Provide example of successful case study utilizing AI and ML in pharmaceutical science and healthcare.
7. What is Digital Safety Data and how is it utilized in the pharmaceutical industry?
8. Define Digital Therapeutics (DTx)?
9. What is E-Prescription and how does it streamline medication management?
10. What is Pharmaceutical Industry 4.0 and how does it integrate digital technologies?

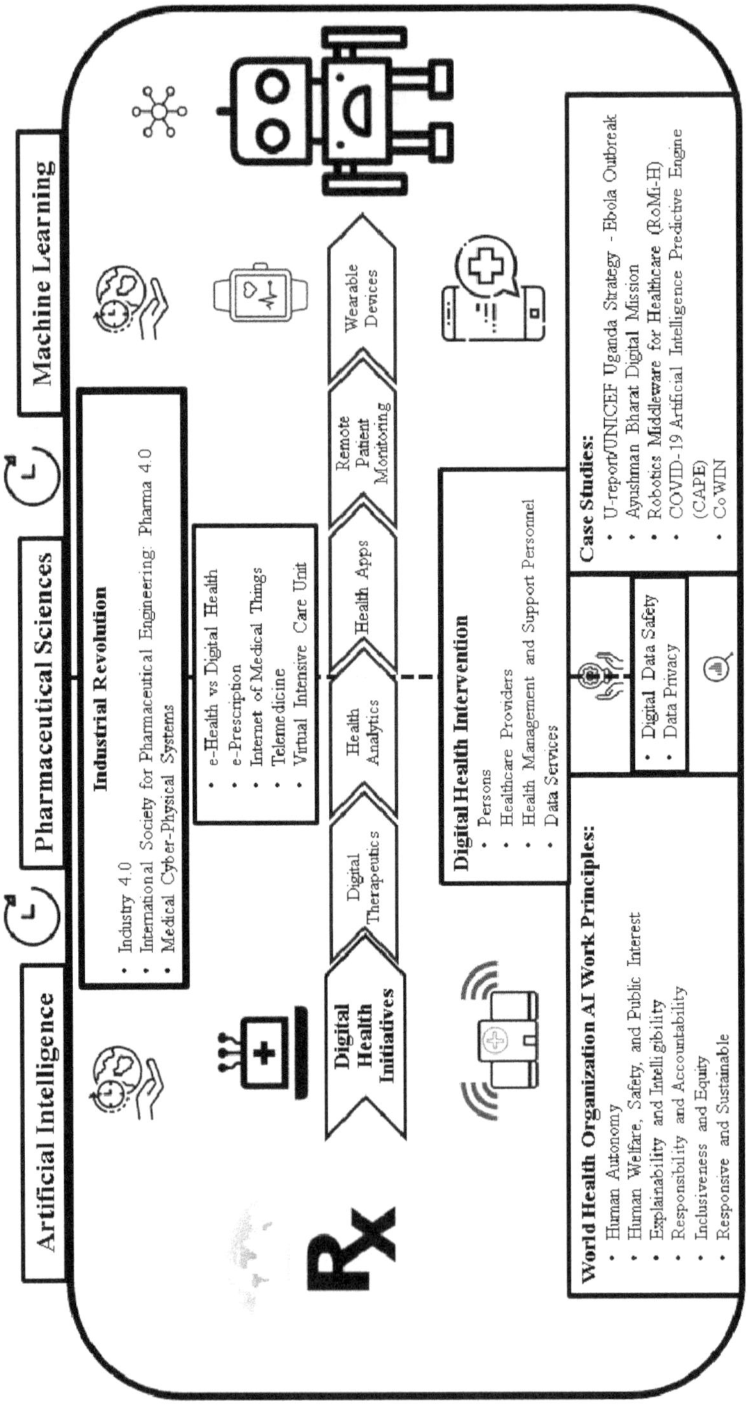
Artificial Intelligence
Pharmaceutical Sciences
Machine Learning
Industrial Revolution
• Industry 4.0
• International Society for Pharmaceutical Engineering: Pharma 4.0
• Medical Cyber-Physical Systems
• e-Health vs Digital Health
• e-Prescription
• Internet of Medical Things
• Telemedicine
• Virtual Intensive Care Unit
Digital Health Initiatives
Digital Therapeutics
Health Analytics
Health Apps
Remote Patient Monitoring
Wearable Devices
Digital Health Intervention
• Persons
• Healthcare Providers
• Health Management and Support Personnel
• Data Services
World Health Organization AI Work Principles:
• Human Autonomy
• Human Welfare, Safety, and Public Interest
• Explainability and Intelligibility
• Responsibility and Accountability
• Inclusiveness and Equity
• Responsive and Sustainable
• Digital Data Safety
• Data Privacy
Case Studies:
• U-report/UNICEF Uganda Strategy - Ebola Outbreak
• Ayushman Bharat Digital Mission
• Robotics Middleware for Healthcare (RoMi-H)
• COVID-19 Artificial Intelligence Predictive Engine (CAPE)
• CoWIN
Rx

Further Readings

1. Aguirre-Sosa, J., & Vargas-Merino, J. A. (2023). Telemedicine Management: Approaches and Perspectives—A Review of the Scientific Literature of the Last 10 Years. *Behavioral Sciences*, *13*(3), 255. https://doi.org/10.3390/bs13030255

2. Ahmad, Z., Rahim, S., Zubair, M., & Abdul-Ghafar, J. (2021). Artificial intelligence (AI) in medicine, current applications and future role with special emphasis on its potential and promise in pathology: Present and future impact, obstacles including costs and acceptance among pathologists, practical and philosophical considerations. A comprehensive review. *Diagnostic Pathology*, *16*(24). https://doi.org/10.1186/s13000-021-01085-4

3. Aldoseri, A., Khalifa, K. N. A. -, & Hamouda, A. M. (2023). Re-Thinking Data Strategy and Integration for Artificial Intelligence: Concepts, Opportunities, and Challenges. *Applied Sciences*, *13*(12), 7082–7082.
https://doi.org/10.3390/ app13127082

4. Alexander, A., Jiang, A., Ferreira, C., & Zurkiya, D. (2020). An Intelligent Future for Medical Imaging: A Market Outlook on Artificial Intelligence for Medical Imaging. *Journal of the American College of Radiology*, *17*(1), 165–170.
https://doi.org/ 10.1016/j.jacr.2019.07.019

5. Alexandre Blanco-González, Cabezón, A., Seco-González, A., Conde-Torres, D., Antelo-Riveiro, P., Ángel Piñeiro, & Garcia-Fandino, R. (2023). The Role of AI in Drug Discovery: Challenges, Opportunities, and Strategies. *The Role of AI in Drug Discovery: Challenges, Opportunities, and Strategies*, *16*(6), 891–891.
https://doi.org/10.3390/ph16060891

6. Alowais, S. A., Alghamdi, S. S., Alsuhebany, N., Alqahtani, T., Abdulrahman Alshaya, Almohareb, S. N., … Albekairy, A. M. (2023). Revolutionizing healthcare: the role of artificial intelligence in clinical practice. *BMC Medical Education*, *23*(1). https://doi.org/10.1186/ s12909-023-04698-z

7. Aria, M., Cuccurullo, C., & Gnasso, A. (2021). A comparison among interpretative proposals for Random Forests. *Machine Learning with Applications*, *6*, 100094. https://doi.org/10.1016/j.mlwa.2021.100094

8. Arnold, C. (2023). Inside the nascent industry of AI-designed drugs. *Nature Medicine*, *29*(6), 1292–1295. https://doi.org/10.1038/s41591-023-02361-0

9. Badwan, B. A., Liaropoulos, G., Kyrodimos, E., Skaltsas, D., Tsirigos, A., & Gorgoulis, V. G. (2023). Machine learning approaches to predict drug efficacy and toxicity in oncology. *Cell Reports Methods*, *3*(2), 100413. https://doi.org/ 10.1016/j.crmeth.2023.100413

10. Bag, S., Dhamija, P., Singh, R. K., Rahman, M. S., & Sreedharan, V. R. (2023). Big data analytics and artificial intelligence technologies based collaborative platform empowering absorptive capacity in health care supply chain: An empirical study. *Journal of Business Research*, *154*, 113315. https://doi.org/10.1016/j.jbusres.2022.113315

11. Bagherian, M., Sabeti, E., Wang, K., Sartor, M. A., Nikolovska-Coleska, Z., & Najarian, K. (2020). Machine learning approaches and databases for prediction of drug–target interaction: a survey paper. *Briefings in Bioinformatics*, *22*(1), 247–269. https://doi.org/10.1093/bib/bbz157

12. Bardy, G. H., Smith, W. M., Hood, M. A., Crozier, I. G., Melton, I. C., Jordaens, L., … Van Gelder, I. C. (2010). An Entirely Subcutaneous Implantable Cardioverter–Defibrillator. *New England Journal of Medicine*, *363*(1), 36–44. https://doi.org/10.1056/nejmoa0909545

13. Barragán-Montero, A., Javaid, U., Valdés, G., Nguyen, D., Desbordes, P., Macq, B., … Lee, J. A. (2021). Artificial intelligence and machine learning for medical imaging: A technology review. *Physica Medica*, *83*, 242–256. https://doi.org/10.1016/j.ejmp.2021.04.016

14. Barredo Arrieta, A., Díaz-Rodríguez, N., Del Ser, J., Bennetot, A., Tabik, S., Barbado, A., … Herrera, F. (2020). Explainable artificial intelligence (XAI): Concepts, taxonomies, opportunities and challenges toward responsible AI. *Information Fusion*, *58*(1), 82–115. Retrieved from https://arxiv.org/pdf/1910.10045.pdf

15. Barrett, A. M., & Baum, S. D. (2016). A model of pathways to artificial superintelligence catastrophe for risk and decision analysis. *Journal of Experimental & Theoretical Artificial Intelligence, 29*(2), 397–414. https://doi.org/10.1080/0952813x.2016.1186228

16. Batool, M., Ahmad, B., & Choi, S. (2019). A Structure-Based Drug Discovery Paradigm. *International Journal of Molecular Sciences, 20*(11), 2783. https://doi.org/10.3390/ijms20112783

17. Bercovich, E., & Javitt, M. C. (2018). Medical Imaging: From Roentgen to the Digital Revolution, and Beyond. *Rambam Maimonides Medical Journal*, *9*(4), e0034. https://doi.org/10.5041/rmmj.10355

18. Bhattamisra, S. K., Banerjee, P., Gupta, P., Mayuren, J., Patra, S., & Candasamy, M. (2023). Artificial Intelligence in Pharmaceutical and Healthcare Research. *Big Data and Cognitive Computing*, *7*(1), 10. https://doi.org/10.3390/bdcc7010010

19. Bittrich, S., Charmi Bhikadiya, Bi, C., Chao, H., Duarte, J. M., Dutta, S., … Rose, Y. (2023). *RCSB Protein Data Bank: Efficient Searching and Simultaneous Access to One Million Computed Structure Models Alongside the PDB Structures Enabled by Architectural Advances. 435*(14), 167994–167994. https://doi.org/10.1016/j.jmb.2023.167994

20. Bohr, A., & Memarzadeh, K. (2020). The rise of artificial intelligence in healthcare applications. *Artificial Intelligence in Healthcare*, *1*(1), 25–60. NCBI. https://doi.org/10.1016/B978-0-12-818438-7.00002-2

21. Busnatu, S., Niculescu, A.-G., Bolocan, A., Octavian Andronic, Anca Pantea Stoian, Alexandru Scafa-Udriște, V. Jinga. (2022). *A Review of Digital Health and Biotelemetry: Modern Approaches towards Personalized Medicine and Remote Health Assessment. 12*(10), 1656–1656. https://doi.org/10.3390/jpm12101656

22. Carpenter, K. A., & Huang, X. (2018). Machine Learning-based Virtual Screening and Its Applications to Alzheimer's Drug Discovery: A Review. *Current Pharmaceutical Design*, *24*(28), 3347–3358. https://doi.org/10.2174/1381612824666180607124038

23. Carracedo-Reboredo, P., Liñares-Blanco, J., Rodríguez-Fernández, N., Cedrón, F., Novoa, F. J., Carballal, A., Fernandez-Lozano, C. (2021). A review on machine learning approaches and trends in drug discovery. *Computational and Structural Biotechnology Journal, 19*, 4538–4558. https://doi.org/10.1016/j.csbj.2021.08.011

24. Cebulla, A., Szpak, Z., Howell, C., Knight, G., & Hussain, S. (2022). Applying ethics to AI in the workplace: the design of a scorecard for Australian workplace health and safety. *AI & SOCIETY*, *38*(38). https://doi.org/10.1007/s00146-022-01460-9

25. Center for Devices and Radiological Health. (2019). Artificial Intelligence and Machine Learning in Software. Retrieved from U.S. Food and Drug Administration website: https://www.fda.gov/medical-devices/software-medical-device-samd/artificial-intelligence-and-machine-learning-software-medical-device

26. Center for Drug Evaluation and Research. (2023). *Artificial Intelligence and machine learning for drug development*. U.S. Food and Drug Administration. https://www.fda.gov/science-research/science-and-research-special-topics/artificial-intelligence-and-machine-learning-aiml-drug-development

27. Chalasani, S. H., Syed, J., Ramesh, M., Patil, V., & Pramod Kumar, T. M. (2023). Artificial intelligence in the field of pharmacy practice: A literature review. *Exploratory Research in Clinical and Social Pharmacy*, *12*, 100346. https://doi.org/10.1016/j.rcsop.2023.100346

28. Charles, M. (2018, June). What is DICOM (Digital Imaging and Communications in Medicine)? - Definition from WhatIs.com. Retrieved from SearchHealthIT website: https://www.techtarget.com/searchhealthit/definition/DICOM-Digital-Imaging-and-Communications-in-Medicine

29. Chatterjee, S., Chaudhuri, R., & Vrontis, D. (2022). AI and digitalization in relationship management: Impact of adopting AI-embedded CRM system. *Journal of Business Research*, *150*, 437–450. https://doi.org/10.1016/j.jbusres.2022.06.033

30. Chavda, V. P., Disha Vihol, Patel, A., Redwan, E. M., & Uversky, V. N. (2023). Introduction to Bioinformatics, AI, and ML for Pharmaceuticals. *Bioinformatics Tools for Pharmaceutical Drug Product Development*, 1–18. https://doi.org/10.1002/9781119865728.ch1

31. Chavda, V., Anand, K., & Apostolopoulos, V. (2023). *Bioinformatics Tools for Pharmaceutical Drug Product Development*. John Wiley & Sons.

32. Chen, J., Swamidass, S. J., Dou, Y., Bruand, J., & Baldi, P. (2005). ChemDB: a public database of small molecules and related chemoinformatics resources. *Bioinformatics*, *21*(22), 4133–4139. https://doi.org/10.1093/bioinformatics/bti683

33. Chen, Q., & Tang, L. (2020). A wearable blood oxygen saturation monitoring system based on bluetooth low energy technology. *Computer Communications*, *160*, 101–110. https://doi.org/10.1016/j.comcom.2020.05.041

34. Chen, W., Liu, X., Zhang, S., & Chen, S. (2023). Artificial Intelligence for Drug Discovery: Resources, Methods, and Applications. *Molecular Therapy - Nucleic Acids*. https://doi.org/10.1016/j.omtn.2023.02.019

35. Chen, X. (2002). TTD: Therapeutic Target Database. *Nucleic Acids Research*, *30*(1), 412–415. https://doi.org/10.1093/nar/30.1.412

36. Chhina, A., Trehan, K., Saini, M., Thakur, S., Kaur, M., Shahtaghi, N. R., … Jain, S. K. (2023). Revolutionizing Pharmaceutical Industry: The Radical Impact of Artificial Intelligence and Machine Learning. *Current Pharmaceutical Design*, *29*(21), 1645–1658. https://doi.org/10.2174/1381612829666230807161421

37. Dagenais, S., Russo, L., Madsen, A., Webster, J., & Becnel, L. (2022). Use of Real-World Evidence to Drive Drug Development Strategy and Inform Clinical Trial Design. *Clinical Pharmacology and Therapeutics*, *111*(1), 77–89. https://doi.org/10.1002/cpt.2480

38. Damiati, S. A. (2020). Digital Pharmaceutical Sciences. *AAPS PharmSciTech*, *21*(6). https://doi.org/10.1208/s12249-020-01747-4

39. Dara, S., Dhamercherla, S., Jadav, S. S., Babu, C. M., & Ahsan, M. J. (2021). Machine Learning in Drug Discovery: A Review. *Artificial Intelligence Review*, *55*(3). https://doi.org/10.1007/s10462-021-10058-4

40. Davenport, T., & Kalakota, R. (2019). The Potential for Artificial Intelligence in Healthcare. *Future Healthcare Journal*, *6*(2), 94–98. https://doi.org/10.7861/futurehosp.6-2-94

41. Doi, K. (2007). Computer-aided diagnosis in medical imaging: Historical review, current status and future potential. *Computerized Medical Imaging and Graphics*, *31*(4-5), 198–211. https://doi.org/10.1016/j.compmedimag.2007.02.002

42. Dwivedi, Y. K., Kshetri, N., Hughes, L., Slade, E. L., Jeyaraj, A., Kar, A. K., … Carter, L. (2023). "So what if ChatGPT wrote it?" Multidisciplinary perspectives on opportunities, challenges and implications of generative conversational AI for research, practice and policy. *International Journal of Information Management*, *71*(0268-4012), 102642. https://doi.org/10.1016/j.ijinfomgt.2023.102642

43. Eloy, C., Marques, A., Pinto, J., Pinheiro, J., Campelos, S., Curado, M., … Polónia, A. (2023). Artificial intelligence–assisted cancer

diagnosis improves the efficiency of pathologists in prostatic biopsies. *Virchows Archiv*. https://doi.org/10.1007/s00428-023-03518-5

44. Fadi Muheidat, & Tawalbeh, L. A. (2023). AIoMT artificial intelligence (AI) and Internet of Medical Things (IoMT). *Elsevier EBooks*, 33–54. https://doi.org/10.1016/b978-0-323-99421-7.00013-1
45. FDA. (2020). *Proposed Regulatory Framework for Modifications to Artificial Intelligence/Machine Learning (AI/ML)-Based Software as a Medical Device (SaMD) -Discussion Paper and Request for Feedback*. Retrieved from https://www.fda.gov/files/medical%20devices/published/US-FDA-Artificial-Intelligence-and-Machine-Learning-Discussion-Paper.pdf
46. Ferrero, E., Brachat, S., Jenkins, J. L., Marc, P., Skewes-Cox, P., Altshuler, R. C., … Stiefl, N. (2020). Ten simple rules to power drug discovery with data science. *PLOS Computational Biology*, *16*(8), e1008126. https://doi.org/10.1371/journal.pcbi.1008126
47. Fjelland, R. (2020). Why general artificial intelligence will not be realized. *Humanities and Social Sciences Communications*, *7*(1). https://doi.org/10.1057/s41599-020-0494-4
48. Flores-Holguín, N., Frau, J., & Glossman-Mitnik, D. (2021). In Silico Pharmacokinetics, ADMET Study and Conceptual DFT Analysis of Two Plant Cyclopeptides Isolated From Rosaceae as a Computational Peptidology Approach. *Frontiers in Chemistry*, *9*. https://doi.org/10.3389/fchem.2021.708364
49. Fürstenau, D., Gersch, M., & Schreiter, S. (2023). Digital Therapeutics (DTx). *Business & Information Systems Engineering*. https://doi.org/10.1007/s12599-023-00804-z
50. Gadekar, R., Sarkar, B., & Gadekar, A. (2020). Assessment of Risks for Successful Implementation of Industry 4.0. *Recent Advances in Computer Science and Communications*, *13*. https://doi.org/10.2174/2666255813999200928215915
51. Gaulton, A., Bellis, L. J., Bento, A. P., Chambers, J., Davies, M., Hersey, A., Overington, J. P. (2011). ChEMBL: a large-scale bioactivity database for drug discovery. *Nucleic Acids Research*, *40*(D1), D1100–D1107. https://doi.org/10.1093/nar/gkr777
52. Ge, A., Gutierrez, E. G., Wook Lee, S., Shah, S., Carmenate, Y., Collard, M., Krauss, G. L. (2022). Seizure triggers identified postictally using a smart watch reporting system. *Epilepsy & Behavior*, *126*, 108472. https://doi.org/10.1016/j.yebeh.2021.108472

53. Ghaffar Nia, N., Kaplanoglu, E., & Nasab, A. (2023). Evaluation of artificial intelligence techniques in disease diagnosis and prediction. *Discover Artificial Intelligence*, *3*(1). https://doi.org/10.1007/s44163-023-00049-5

54. Gilbert, S., Anderson, S., Daumer, M., Li, P., Melvin, T., & Williams, R. (2023). Learning From Experience and Finding the Right Balance in the Governance of Artificial Intelligence and Digital Health Technologies. *Journal of Medical Internet Research*, *25*(1), e43682. https://doi.org/10.2196/43682

55. Go, H. (2022). Digital Pathology and Artificial Intelligence Applications in Pathology. *Brain Tumor Research and Treatment*, *10*(2), 76. https://doi.org/10.14791/btrt.2021.0032

56. Gobble, M. M. (2019). The Road to Artificial General Intelligence. *Research-Technology Management*, *62*(3), 55–59. https://doi.org/10.1080/08956308.2019.1587336

57. Goh, G. D., Sing, S. L., & Yeong, W. Y. (2020). A review on machine learning in 3D printing: applications, potential, and challenges. *Artificial Intelligence Review*, *54*(1), 63–94. https://doi.org/10.1007/s10462-020-09876-9

58. *Government of India launches ArogyaSetu app to track Covid 19 infection*. Press Information Bureau. (n.d.). https://pib.gov.in/PressReleaseIframePage.aspx?PRID=1610326

59. Gowda, V., Jordan, S. G., & Awan, O. A. (2021). Artificial Intelligence in Radiology Education: A Longitudinal Approach. *Academic Radiology*. https://doi.org/10.1016/j.acra.2021.08.022

60. Griffith, M., Griffith, O. L., Coffman, A. C., Weible, J. V., McMichael, J. F., Spies, N. C., … Smith, S. M. (2013). DGIdb: mining the druggable genome. *Nature Methods*, *10*(12), 1209–1210. https://doi.org/10.1038/nmeth.2689

61. Grooby, E., Sitaula, C., Chang Kwok, T., Sharkey, D., Marzbanrad, F., & Malhotra, A. (2023). Artificial Intelligence-Driven Wearable Technologies for neonatal cardiorespiratory monitoring: Part 1 wearable technology. *Pediatric Research*, *93*(2), 413–425. https://doi.org/1038/s41390-022-02416-x

62. Gunasekeran, D.V. *et al.* (2021) 'Applications of digital health for public health responses to covid-19: A systematic scoping review of artificial intelligence, telehealth and Related Technologies', *npj Digital Medicine*, 4(1). https://doi.org/10.1038/s41746-021-00412-9.

63. Guo, Y., Chen, M., Yang, L., Yin, H., Yang, H., & Zhou, Y. (2024). A neural network with a human learning paradigm for breast fibroadenoma segmentation in sonography. *BioMedical Engineering Online*, *23*(1). https://doi.org/10.1186/s12938-024-01198-z

64. Gupta, R., Srivastava, D., Sahu, M., Tiwari, S., Ambasta, R. K., & Kumar, P. (2021). Artificial intelligence to deep learning: machine intelligence approach for drug discovery. *Molecular Diversity*, *25*(3), 1–46. https://doi.org/10.1007/s11030-021-10217-3

65. Haleem, A., Javaid, M., Singh, R. P., & Suman, R. (2021). Telemedicine for healthcare: Capabilities, features, barriers, and applications. *Sensors International*, *2*(2). https://doi.org/10.1016/j.sintl.2021.100117

66. Han, R., Yoon, H., Kim, G., Lee, H., & Lee, Y. (2023). Revolutionizing Medicinal Chemistry: The Application of Artificial Intelligence (AI) in Early Drug Discovery. *Pharmaceuticals*, *16*(9), 1259. https://doi.org/10.3390/ph16091259

67. Han, Y., & Tao, J. (2024). Revolutionizing Pharma: Unveiling the AI and LLM Trends in the Pharmaceutical Industry. *ArXiv (Cornell University)*. https://doi.org/10.48550/arxiv.2401.10273

68. Harrison, J. H., Gilbertson, J. R., Hanna, M. G., Olson, N. H., Seheult, J. N., Sorace, J. M., & Stram, M. N. (2021). Introduction to Artificial Intelligence and Machine Learning for Pathology. *Archives of Pathology & Laboratory Medicine*. https://doi.org/10.5858/arpa.2020-0541-cp

69. Hoang, M. L., Carratù, M., Paciello, V., & Pietrosanto, A. (2021). Body Temperature—Indoor Condition Monitor and Activity Recognition by MEMS Accelerometer Based on IoT-Alert System for People in Quarantine Due to COVID-19. *Sensors*, *21*(7), 2313. https://doi.org/10.3390/s21072313

70. Hole, G., Hole, A. S., & Shaw, I. M. (2021). Digitalization in pharmaceutical industry: What to focus on under the digital implementation process? *International Journal of Pharmaceutics: X*, *3*, 100095. Sciencedirect. https://doi.org/10.1016/j.ijpx.2021.100095

71. Homeyer, A., Lotz, J., Schwen, L. O., Weiss, N., Romberg, D., Höfener, H., … Hufnagl, P. (2021). Artificial Intelligence in Pathology: From Prototype to Product. *Journal of Pathology Informatics*, *12*, 13. https://doi.org/10.4103/jpi.jpi_84_20

72. Huang, S. (2018). Applications of Support Vector Machine (SVM) Learning in Cancer Genomics. *Cancer Genomics & Proteomics*, *15*(1). https://doi.org/10.21873/cgp.20063

73. Huma, T., & Peng, Z. (2023). Introduction to Regulatory Affairs and Different Regulatory Bodies for Pharmaceutical Products and Impact of Digitalization on Regulatory Affairs. *Pharmacology & Pharmacy*, *14*(11), 463–477. https://doi.org/10.4236/pp.2023.1411030

74. Jahn, A. S., Navarini, A. A., Cerminara, S. E., Kostner, L., Huber, S. M., Kunz, M., … Maul, L. V. (2022). Over-Detection of Melanoma-Suspect Lesions by a CE-Certified Smartphone App: Performance in Comparison to Dermatologists, 2D and 3D Convolutional Neural Networks in a Prospective Data Set of 1204 Pigmented Skin Lesions Involving Patients' Perception. *Cancers*, *14*(15), 3829. https://doi.org/10.3390/cancers14153829

75. Jarab, A. S., Shrouq Abu Heshmeh, & Al, A. Z. (2023). Barriers to AI in pharmacy practice. *Journal of Medical Economics*, 1–9. https://doi.org/10.1080/13696998.2023.2265245

76. Jimmy, B., & Jose, J. (2011). Patient Medication Adherence: Measures in Daily Practice. *Oman Medical Journal*, *26*(3), 155–159. https://doi.org/10.5001/omj.2011.38

77. Jin, D., Harrison, A. P., Zhang, L., Yan, K., Wang, Y., Cai, J., … Lu, L. (2021). Artificial intelligence in radiology. *Artificial Intelligence in Medicine*, 265–289. https://doi.org/10.1016/b978-0-12-821259-2.00014-4

78. Jin, X., Liu, C., Xu, T., Su, L., & Zhang, X. (2020). Artificial intelligence biosensors: Challenges and prospects. *Biosensors and Bioelectronics*, *165*, 112412. https://doi.org/10.1016/j.bios.2020.112412

79. Jing, Y., Bian, Y., Hu, Z., Wang, L., & Xie, X.-Q. S. (2018). Deep Learning for Drug Design: an Artificial Intelligence Paradigm for Drug Discovery in the Big Data Era. *The AAPS Journal*, *20*(3). https://doi.org/10.1208/s12248-018-0210-0

80. Johnson, K. B., Wei, W., Weeraratne, D., Frisse, M. E., Misulis, K., Rhee, K., … Snowdon, J. L. (2020). Precision Medicine, AI, and the Future of Personalized Health Care. *Clinical and Translational Science*, *14*(1). Retrieved from https://www.ncbi.nlm.nih.gov/pmc/articles/PMC7877825/

81. Joseph Bamdele Awotunde, Chakraborty, C., AbdulRaheem, M., Rasheed Gbenga Jimoh, Idowu Dauda Oladipo, & Akash Kumar Bhoi. (2023). Internet of medical things for enhanced smart healthcare systems. *Elsevier EBooks*, 1–28. https://doi.org/10.1016/b978-0-323-91916-6.00009-6

82. Kasula, B. Y. (2024). Ethical Implications and Future Prospects of Artificial Intelligence in Healthcare: A Research Synthesis. *International Meridian Journal*, *6*(6), 1–7. Retrieved from https://meridianjournal.in/index.php/IMJ/article/view/31

83. Kavasidis, I., Lallas, E., Leligkou, H. C., Oikonomidis, G., Karydas, D., Gerogiannis, V. C., & Karageorgos, A. (2023). Deep Transformers for Computing and Predicting ALCOA+Data Integrity Compliance in the Pharmaceutical Industry. *Applied Sciences*, *13*(13), NA–NA. https://doi.org/10.3390/app13137616

84. Kazi Asraf Ali, SK Mohin, Mondal, P., Goswami, S., Ghosh, S., & Sabyasachi Choudhuri. (2024). Influence of artificial intelligence in modern pharmaceutical formulation and drug development. *Future Journal of Pharmaceutical Sciences (Print)*, *10*(1). https://doi.org/10.1186/s43094-024-00625-1

85. Kaul, V., Enslin, S. and Gross, S.A. (2020) 'History of artificial intelligence in medicine', *Gastrointestinal Endoscopy*, 92(4), pp. 807–812. https://doi.org/10.1016/j.gie.2020.06.040.

86. Keenan, A. B., Jenkins, S. L., Jagodnik, K. M., Koplev, S., He, E., Torre, D., … Schürer, S. C. (2018). The Library of Integrated Network-Based Cellular Signatures NIH Program: System-Level Cataloging of Human Cells Response to Perturbations. *Cell Systems*, *6*(1), 13–24. https://doi.org/10.1016/j.cels.2017.11.001

87. Ker, J., Wang, L., Rao, J., & Lim, T. (2018). Deep Learning Applications in Medical Image Analysis. *IEEE Access*, *6*, 9375–9389. https://doi.org/10.1109/ACCESS.2017.2788044

88. Khan, O., Parvez, M., Kumari, P., Parvez, S., & Ahmad, S. (2023). The future of pharmacy: How AI is revolutionizing the industry. *Intelligent Pharmacy*, *1*(1), 32–40. https://doi.org/10.1016/j.ipha.2023.04.008

89. Khan, R. (2022). Effectiveness of tens therapy for pain management by physical therapists working in tertiary care hospitals of karachi. *Pakistan Journal of Rehabilitation*, *11*(2), 13–21. https://doi.org/10.36283/pjr.zu.11.2/004

90. Khanna, V. V., Chadaga, K., Sampathila, N., Prabhu, S., & P., R. C. (2023). A machine learning and explainable artificial intelligence triage-prediction system for COVID-19. *Decision Analytics Journal*, 100246. https://doi.org/10.1016/j.dajour.2023.100246

91. Kim, I., Kang, K., Song, Y., & Kim, T.-J. (2022). Application of Artificial Intelligence in Pathology: Trends and Challenges. *Diagnostics*, *12*(11), 2794. https://doi.org/10.3390/diagnostics12112794

92. Kim, S., Chow, B. C., Park, S., & Liu, H. (2023). The Usage of Digital Health Technology Among Older Adults in Hong Kong and the Role of Technology Readiness and eHealth Literacy: Path Analysis. *Journal of Medical Internet Research*, *25*, e41915. https://doi.org/10.2196/41915

93. Kim, S., Thiessen, P. A., Bolton, E. E., Chen, J., Fu, G., Gindulyte, A., … Bryant, S. H. (2015). PubChem Substance and Compound databases. *Nucleic Acids Research*, *44*(D1), D1202–D1213. https://doi.org/10.1093/nar/gkv951

94. Kolluri, S., Lin, J., Liu, R., Zhang, Y., & Zhang, W. (2022). Machine Learning and Artificial Intelligence in Pharmaceutical Research and Development: a Review. *The AAPS Journal*, *24*(1). https://doi.org/10.1208/s12248-021-00644-3

95. Kothari, R., Sahab, S., Singh, H. M., Singh, R. P., Singh, B., Pathania, D., … Tyagi, V. V. (2021). COVID-19 and waste management in Indian scenario: challenges and possible solutions. *Environmental Science and Pollution Research*, *28*(38), 52702–52723. https://doi.org/10.1007/s11356-021-15028-5

96. Kuhn, M., Letunic, I., Jensen, L. J., & Bork, P. (2015). The SIDER database of drugs and side effects. *Nucleic Acids Research*, *44*(D1), D1075–D1079. https://doi.org/10.1093/nar/gkv1075

97. Kumar, A., Mani, V., Jain, V., Gupta, H., & Venkatesh, V. G. (2022). Managing healthcare supply chain through Artificial Intelligence (AI): A study of critical success factors. *Computers & Industrial Engineering*, *175*, 108815. https://doi.org/10.1016/j.cie.2022.108815

98. Lee, D., & Yoon, S. N. (2021). Application of Artificial Intelligence-Based Technologies in the Healthcare Industry: Opportunities and Challenges. *International Journal of Environmental Research and Public Health*, *18*(1), 271. mdpi. Retrieved from https://www.mdpi.com/1660-4601/18/1/271

99. Li, F., Liu, Z., Chen, H., Jiang, M., Zhang, X., & Wu, Z. (2019). Automatic Detection of Diabetic Retinopathy in Retinal Fundus Photographs Based on Deep Learning Algorithm. *Translational Vision Science & Technology*, *8*(6), 4. https://doi.org/10.1167/tvst.8.6.4

100. Liao, K.-M., Liu, C.-F., Chen, C.-J., Feng, J.-Y., Shu, C.-C., & Ma, Y.-S. (2023). *Using an Artificial Intelligence Approach to Predict the Adverse Effects and Prognosis of Tuberculosis. 13*(6), 1075–1075. https://doi.org/10.3390/diagnostics13061075

101. Lim, S., Lee, S., Piao, Y., Choi, M., Bang, D., Gu, J., & Kim, S. (2022). On modeling and utilizing chemical compound information with deep learning technologies: A task-oriented approach. *Computational and Structural Biotechnology Journal*, *20*, 4288–4304. https://doi.org/10.1016/j.csbj.2022.07.049

102. Liu, F., Zhou, Z., Samsonov, A., Blankenbaker, D., Larison, W., Kanarek, A., … Kijowski, R. (2018). Deep Learning Approach for Evaluating Knee MR Images: Achieving High Diagnostic Performance for Cartilage Lesion Detection. *Radiology*, *289*(1), 160–169. https://doi.org/10.1148/radiol.2018172986

103. Liu, Z., Roberts, R. A., Lal-Nag, M., Chen, X., Huang, R., & Tong, W. (2021). AI-based language models powering drug discovery and development. *Drug Discovery Today*, *26*(11), 2593–2607. https://doi.org/10.1016/j.drudis.2021.06.009

104. Lu, M. *et al.* (2023) 'Artificial Intelligence in pharmaceutical sciences', *Engineering*, 27, pp. 37–69. https://doi.org/10.1016/j.eng.2023.01.014.

105. Madhukar, N. S., Khade, P. K., Huang, L., Gayvert, K., Galletti, G., Stogniew, M., Elemento, O. (2019). A Bayesian machine learning approach for drug target identification using diverse data types. *Nature Communications*, *10*(1). https://doi.org/10.1038/s41467-019-12928-6

106. Mahdi, S. S., Battineni, G., Khawaja, M., Allana, R., Siddiqui, M. K., & Agha, D. (2023). How does artificial intelligence impact digital healthcare initiatives? A review of AI applications in dental healthcare. *International Journal of Information Management Data Insights*, *3*(1), 100144. https://doi.org/10.1016/j.jjimei.2022.100144

107. Malta, T. M., Sokolov, A., Gentles, A. J., Burzykowski, T., Poisson, L., Weinstein, J. N., Hoadley, K. A. (2018). Machine Learning Identifies Stemness Features Associated with Oncogenic Dedifferentiation. *Cell*, *173*(2), 338-354.e15. https://doi.org/10.1016/j.cell.2018.03.034

108. Manzano, T., & Langer, G. (2018). *GETTING READY FOR PHARMA 4.0 Data integrity in cloud and big data applications*. Retrieved from https://www.ispe.gr.jp/ISPE/02_katsudou/pdf/201812_en.pdf

109. Manzoni, C., Kia, D. A., Vandrovcova, J., Hardy, J., Wood, N. W., Lewis, P. A., & Ferrari, R. (2016). Genome, transcriptome and proteome: the rise of omics data and their integration in biomedical sciences. *Briefings in Bioinformatics*, *19*(2), 286–302. https://doi.org/10.1093/bib/bbw114

110. Maojo, V., & Kulikowski, C. A. (2003). Bioinformatics and Medical Informatics: Collaborations on the Road to Genomic Medicine? *Journal of the American Medical Informatics Association*, *10*(6), 515–522. https://doi.org/10.1197/jamia.m1305

111. Maryna Stasevych, & Viktor Zvarych. (2023). Innovative Robotic Technologies and Artificial Intelligence in Pharmacy and Medicine: Paving the Way for the Future of Health Care—A Review. *Big Data and Cognitive Computing*, *7*(3), 147–147. https://doi.org/10.3390/bdcc7030147

112. Mbunge, E. *et al.* (2021) 'Sensors and healthcare 5.0: Transformative SHIFT IN virtual care through Emerging Digital Health Technologies', *Global Health Journal*, 5(4), pp. 169–177. https://doi.org/10.1016/j.glohj.2021.11.008.

113. Mehta, M. (2021). *Tracking and Preventing Diseases with Artificial Intelligence*. Springer Nature.

114. Mohsen, F., Ali, H., El Hajj, N., & Shah, Z. (2022). Artificial intelligence-based methods for fusion of electronic health records and imaging data. *Scientific Reports*, *12*(1), 17981. https://doi.org/10.1038/s41598-022-22514-4

115. N. S. D., Pai, R. M., Bhat, S. N., & Pai, M. (2024). Deep learning-based automated spine fracture type identification with clinically validated GAN generated CT images. *Cogent Engineering*, *11*(1). https://doi.org/10.1080/23311916.2023.2295645

116. Najjar, R. (2023). Redefining Radiology: A Review of Artificial Intelligence Integration in Medical Imaging. *Diagnostics*, *13*(17), 2760. https://doi.org/10.3390/diagnostics13172760

117. Nayarisseri, A. (2021). Artificial Intelligence, Big Data and Machine Learning Approaches in Precision Medicine & Drug Discovery. *Current Drug Targets*, *22*(6), 631–655. https://doi.org/10.2174/18735592mtezsmdmnz

118. Netherton, T. J., Cardenas, C. E., Rhee, D. J., Court, L. E., & Beadle, B. M. (2020). The Emergence of Artificial Intelligence within Radiation Oncology Treatment Planning. *Oncology*, *99*(2), 124–134. https://doi.org/10.1159/000512172

119. Niazi, S. K. (2023). The Coming of Age of AI/ML in Drug Discovery, Development, Clinical Testing, and Manufacturing: The FDA Perspectives. *Drug Design Development and Therapy, Volume 17*, 2691–2725. https://doi.org/10.2147/dddt.s424991

120. Niculescu, A.-G., Bolocan, A., Petrescu, G., & Abedi, V. (2022). Citation. *J. Clin. Med, 2022*, 2265. https://doi.org/10.3390/jcm11082265

121. Nikola Savanović, Toskovic, A., A. Martin Petrovic, Miodrag Živković, Robertas Damaševičius, Jovanovic, L., … Boško Nikolić. (2023). Intrusion Detection in Healthcare 4.0 Internet of Things Systems via Metaheuristics Optimized Machine Learning. *Sustainability*, *15*(16), 12563–12563. https://doi.org/10.3390/su151612563

122. Ninduwezuor-Ehiobu, N., Tula, O. A., Daraojimba, C., Ofonagoro, K. A., Ogunjobi, O. A., Gidiagba, J. O., … Banso, A. A. (2023). Tracing the evolution of ai and machine learning applications in advancing materials discovery and production processes. *Engineering Science & Technology Journal*, *4*(3), 66–83. https://doi.org/10.51594/estj.v4i3.552

123. Nosrati, H., & Nosrati, M. (2023). Artificial Intelligence in Regenerative Medicine: Applications and Implications. *Biomimetics*, *8*(5), 442. https://doi.org/10.3390/biomimetics8050442

124. NV, S. (2024). Pharma 4.0: Key Steps and Real World Applications | Scilife. Retrieved May 27, 2024, from www.scilife.io website: https://www.scilife.io/glossary/pharma-4

125. Nyangaresi, V. O., El-Omari, N. K. T., & Nyakina, J. N. (2022). Efficient Feature Selection and ML Algorithm for Accurate Diagnostics. *Journal of Computer Science Research*, *4*(1), 10–19. https://doi.org/10.30564/jcsr.v4i1.3852

126. Ogbuke, N. J., Yusuf, Y. Y., Dharma, K., & Mercangoz, B. A. (2020). Big data supply chain analytics: ethical, privacy and security challenges posed to business, industries and society. *Production Planning & Control*, *33*(2-3), 1–15. Retrieved from https://www.tandfonline.com/doi/abs/10.1080/09537287.2020.1810764

127. Olawade, D. B., David-Olawade, A. C., Wada, O. Z., Asaolu, A. J., Adereni, T., & Ling, J. (2024). Artificial intelligence in healthcare delivery: Prospects and pitfalls. *Journal of Medicine, Surgery, and Public Health*, *3*, 100108. https://doi.org/10.1016/j.glmedi.2024.100108

128. Olla, P., & Tan, J. (2022). *Digital Health Care: Perspectives, Applications, and Cases*. Jones & Bartlett Learning.

129. Patel, L., Shukla, T., Huang, X., Ussery, D. W., & Wang, S. (2020). Machine Learning Methods in Drug Discovery. *Molecules*, *25*(22), 5277. https://doi.org/10.3390/molecules25225277

130. Patel, V., & Shah, M. (2021). A comprehensive study on artificial intelligence and machine learning in drug discovery and drug development. *Intelligent Medicine*, *2*(3). https://doi.org/10.1016/j.imed.2021.10.001

131. Paul, D., Sanap, G., Shenoy, S., Kalyane, D., Kalia, K., & Tekade, R. K. (2020). Artificial intelligence in drug discovery and development. *Drug Discovery Today*, *26*(1). ncbi. https://doi.org/10.1016/j.drudis.2020.10.010

132. Petrick, N., Chen, W., Delfino, J. G., Gallas, B. D., Kang, Y., Krainak, D., … Samala, R. K. (2023). Regulatory considerations for medical imaging AI/ML devices in the United States: concepts and challenges. *Journal of Medical Imaging*, *10*(05). https://doi.org/10.1117/1.jmi.10.5.051804

133. Pramanik, P. K. D., Upadhyaya, B. K., Pal, S., & Pal, T. (2019). Internet of things, smart sensors, and pervasive systems: Enabling connected and pervasive healthcare. *Healthcare Data Analytics and Management*, 1–58. https://doi.org/10.1016/b978-0-12-815368-0.00001-4

134. Pruvo, J. P., Luciani, A., Boyer, L., & Bartoli, J.-M. . (2020). Tomorrow's medical imaging builds on today's foundations - Prevention, care and innovation at the service of patients: A program for radiology and medical imaging. *Diagnostic and Interventional Imaging*, *101*(3), 123–125. https://doi.org/10.1016/j.diii.2019.12.003

135. Pujari, S., Reis, A., Zhao, Y., Alsalamah, S., Serhan, F., Reeder, J. C., & Labrique, A. B. (2023). Artificial intelligence for global health: cautious optimism with safeguards. *Bulletin of the World Health Organization*, *101*(6), 364. https://doi.org/10.2471/BLT.23.290215

136. Pun, F. W., Ozerov, I. V., & Zhavoronkov, A. (2023). AI-powered therapeutic target discovery. *Trends in Pharmacological Sciences*, *44*(9), 561–572. https://doi.org/10.1016/j.tips.2023.06.010

137. Qiu, H., Qiu, M., Liu, M., & Memmi, G. (2020). Secure Health Data Sharing for Medical Cyber-Physical Systems for the Healthcare 4.0. *IEEE Journal of Biomedical and Health Informatics*, *24*(9), 2499–2505. https://doi.org/10.1109/jbhi.2020.2973467

138. Qureshi, R., Irfan, M., Taimoor Muzaffar Gondal, Khan, S., Wu, J., Muhammad Usman Hadi., Alam, T. (2023). AI in Drug Discovery and its Clinical Relevance. *Heliyon*, *9*(7), e17575–e17575. https://doi.org/10.1016/j.heliyon.2023.e17575

139. Rathore, A. S., Nikita, S., Thakur, G., & Mishra, S. (2022). Artificial intelligence and machine learning applications in biopharmaceutical manufacturing. *Trends in Biotechnology*, *41*(4). https://doi.org/10.1016/j.tibtech.2022.08.007

140. Raza, M. A., Aziz, S., Noreen, M., Saeed, A., Anjum, I., Ahmed, M., & Raza, S. M. (2022). Artificial Intelligence (AI) in Pharmacy: An Overview of Innovations. *INNOVATIONS in Pharmacy*, *13*(2), 13. https://doi.org/10.24926/iip.v13i2.4839

141. Rodgers, W., Murray, J. M., Stefanidis, A., Degbey, W. Y., & Tarba, S. Y. (2022). An artificial intelligence algorithmic approach to ethical decision-making in human resource management processes. *Human Resource Management Review*, *33*(1), 100925. Retrieved from https://www.sciencedirect.com/science/article/pii/S1053482222000432

142. Rodríguez-Pérez, R., & Bajorath, J. (2022). Evolution of Support Vector Machine and Regression Modeling in Chemoinformatics and Drug Discovery. *Journal of Computer-Aided Molecular Design*, *36*(5), 355–362. https://doi.org/10.1007/s10822-022-00442-9

143. Sadybekov, A.V. and Katritch, V. (2023) 'Computational approaches Streamlining Drug Discovery', *Nature*, 616(7958), pp. 673–685. https://doi.org/10.1038/s41586-023-05905-z

144. Sahu, A., Mishra, J., & Kushwaha, N. (2021). Artificial Intelligence (AI) in Drugs and Pharmaceuticals. *Combinatorial Chemistry & High Throughput Screening*, *25*. https://doi.org/10.2174/1386207325666211207153943

145. Sai, S., & Vinay Chamola. (2024). AI-assisted Blockchain-enabled Smart and Secure E-prescription Management Framework. *ACM Transactions on Internet Technology*. https://doi.org/10.1145/3641279

146. Sarath Kumar Boddu, R., Ahamad, S., Pradeep Kumar, K. V., Ramalingam, M., Kirana Pallathadka, L., & Peniero Tupas, F. (2022). Analysis of Robotics, Artificial intelligence and Machine learning in the field of healthcare sector. *Materials Today: Proceedings*, *56*, 2323–2327. https://doi.org/10.1016/j.matpr.2021.12.016

147. Sarhadi, V. K., & Armengol, G. (2022). Molecular Biomarkers in Cancer. *Biomolecules*, *12*(8), 1021. https://doi.org/10.3390/biom12081021

148. Sarkar, C., Das, B., Rawat, V. S., Wahlang, J. B., Nongpiur, A., Tiewsoh, I., … Sony, H. T. (2023). Artificial Intelligence and Machine Learning Technology Driven Modern Drug Discovery and Development. *International Journal of Molecular Sciences*, *24*(3), 2026. https://doi.org/10.3390/ijms24032026

149. Scalvini, S., Vitacca, M., Paletta, L., Giordano, A., & Balbi, B. (2004). Telemedicine: a new frontier for effective healthcare services. *Monaldi Archives for Chest Disease*, *61*(4). https://doi.org/10.4081/monaldi.2004.686

150. Schork, N. J. (2019). Artificial Intelligence and Personalized Medicine. *Precision Medicine in Cancer Therapy*, *178*, 265–283. https://doi.org/10.1007/978-3-030-16391-4_11

151. Sevakula, R. K., Au-Yeung, W. M., Singh, J. P., Heist, E. K., Isselbacher, E. M., & Armoundas, A. A. (2020). State-of-the-Art Machine Learning Techniques Aiming to Improve Patient Outcomes Pertaining to the Cardiovascular System. *Journal of the American Heart Association*, *9*(4). https://doi.org/10.1161/jaha.119.013924

152. Shabbir Syed-Abdul, Luis Fernandez Luque, Pei-Yun Sabrina Hsueh, García-Gomez, J. M., & Begoña Garcia-Zapirain. (2020). *Data Analytics and Applications of the Wearable Sensors in Healthcare*. MDPI.

153. Sharma, R. S., Rohatgi, A., Jain, S., & Singh, D. (2023). The Ayushman Bharat Digital Mission (ABDM): making of India's Digital Health Story. *CSI Transactions on ICT*, *11*(1). https://doi.org/10.1007/s40012-023-00375-0

154. Siemers, F. M., Feldmann, C., & Bajorath, J. (2022). Minimal data requirements for accurate compound activity prediction using machine learning methods of different complexity. *Cell Reports Physical Science*, 101113. https://doi.org/10.1016/j.xcrp.2022.101113

155. SingHealth Group. (2023). Retrieved May 27, 2024, from www.cgh.com.sg website: https://www.cgh.com.sg/chart/Documents/RoMi-H%20CHART%20Framework.pdf

156. Singh, S., Kumar, R., Payra, S., Singh, S. K., Singh, S., Kumar, R., … Singh, S. K. (2023). Artificial Intelligence and Machine Learning in Pharmacological Research: Bridging the Gap Between Data and Drug Discovery. *Cureus*, *15*(8). https://doi.org/10.7759/cureus.44359

157. Song, X., Chen, E., & Zhang, Y. (2023). Integrated Molecular Modeling and Machine Learning for Drug Design. *PubMed*. https://doi.org/10.1021/acs.jctc.3c00814

158. Tagde, P., Tagde, S., Bhattacharya, T., Tagde, P., Chopra, H., Akter, R., … Rahman, Md. H. (2021). Blockchain and artificial intelligence technology in e-Health. *Environmental Science and Pollution Research*, *28*(38), 52810–52831. https://doi.org/10.1007/s11356-021-16223-0

159. Tamanna Sharma, Abhinav Mankoo, & Vivek Sood. (2021). Artificial intelligence in advanced pharmacy. *International Journal of Science and Research Archive*, *2*(1), 047–054. https://doi.org/10.30574/ijsra.2021.2.1.0301

160. Tang, C., Ji, J., Tang, Y., Gao, S., Tang, Z., & Todo, Y. (2020). A novel machine learning technique for computer-aided diagnosis. *Engineering Applications of Artificial Intelligence*, *92*, 103627. https://doi.org/10.1016/j.engappai.2020.103627

161. Tang, X. (2020). The role of artificial intelligence in medical imaging research. *BJR|Open*, *2*(1), 20190031. https://doi.org/10.1259/bjro.20190031

162. Tanil, C. T., & Yong, M. H. (2020). Mobile phones: The effect of its presence on learning and memory. *PLOS ONE*, *15*(8), e0219233. https://doi.org/10.1371/journal.pone.0219233

163. Taylor, D. (2019). The Pharmaceutical Industry and the Future of Drug Development. *Issues in Environmental Science and Technology*, *1*(1), 1–33. https://doi.org/10.1039/9781782622345-00001

164. Terranova, N., Venkatakrishnan, K., & Benincosa, L. J. (2021). Application of Machine Learning in Translational Medicine: Current Status and Future Opportunities. *The AAPS Journal*, *23*(4). https://doi.org/10.1208/s12248-021-00593-x

165. Thapa, C., & Camtepe, S. (2021). Precision health data: Requirements, challenges and existing techniques for data security and privacy. *Computers in Biology and Medicine*, *129*(1). https://doi.org/10.1016/j.compbiomed.2020.104130

166. Tingle, B. I., Tang, K. G., Castanon, M., Gutierrez, J. J., Munkhzul Khurelbaatar, Chinzorig Dandarchuluun, … Irwin, J. J. (2023). *ZINC-22—A Free Multi-Billion-Scale Database of Tangible Compounds for Ligand Discovery*. *63*(4), 1166–1176. https://doi.org/10.1021/acs.jcim.2c01253

167. Turón, G., Hlozek, J., Woodland, J. G., Chibale, K., & Duran-Frigola, M. (2022). First fully-automated AI/ML virtual screening cascade implemented at a drug discovery centre in Africa. *BioRxiv (Cold Spring Harbor Laboratory)*. https://doi.org/10.1101/2022.12.13.520154

168. Tuyet, T., Agung Surya Wibowo, Hilal Tayara, & Kil To Chong. (2023). Artificial Intelligence in Drug Toxicity Prediction: Recent Advances, Challenges, and Future Perspectives. *Journal of Chemical Information and Modeling*. https://doi.org/10.1021/acs.jcim.3c00200

169. Varadi, M., Anyango, S., Deshpande, M., Nair, S., Natassia, C., Yordanova, G., Figurnov, M. (2021). AlphaFold Protein Structure Database: massively expanding the structural coverage of protein-sequence space with high-accuracy models. *Nucleic Acids Research*, *50*(D1). https://doi.org/10.1093/nar/gkab1061

170. Vatansever, S., Schlessinger, A., Wacker, D., Kaniskan, H. Ü., Jin, J., Zhou, M., & Zhang, B. (2020). Artificial intelligence and machine learning-aided drug discovery in central nervous system diseases: State-of-the-arts and future directions. *Medicinal Research Reviews*, *41*(3), 1427–1473. https://doi.org/10.1002/med.21764

171. Vijayan, R. S. K., Kihlberg, J., Cross, J. B., & Poongavanam, V. (2021). Enhancing preclinical drug discovery with artificial intelligence. *Drug Discovery Today*, *27*(4). https://doi.org/10.1016/j.drudis.2021.11.023

172. *Virtual screening: Computational chemistry: Biopharma: Aganitha*. Aganitha AI Inc. (2024, April 10). https://www.aganitha.ai/solutions/virtual-screening/

173. Vishnoi, S., Matre, H., Garg, P., & Pandey, S. K. (2020). Artificial intelligence and machine learning for protein toxicity prediction using proteomics data. *Chemical Biology & Drug Design*, *96*(3), 902–920. https://doi.org/10.1111/cbdd.13701

174. Volkamer, A., Riniker, S., Nittinger, E., Lanini, J., Grisoni, F., Evertsson, E., … Schneider, N. (2023). Machine learning for small molecule drug discovery in academia and industry. *Artificial Intelligence in the Life Sciences*, *3*, 100056. https://doi.org/10.1016/j.ailsci.2022.100056

175. Vora, L. K., Gholap, A. D., Jetha, K., Thakur, R. R. S., Solanki, H. K., & Chavda, V. P. (2023). Artificial Intelligence in Pharmaceutical Technology and Drug Delivery Design. *Pharmaceutics*, *15*(7), 1916–1916. https://doi.org/10.3390/pharmaceutics15071916

176. Wishart, D. S., Knox, C., Guo, A. C., Shrivastava, S., Hassanali, M., Stothard, P., Woolsey, J. (2006). DrugBank: a comprehensive resource for in silico drug discovery and exploration. *Nucleic Acids Research*, *34*(Database issue), D668-72. https://doi.org/10.1093/nar/gkj067

177. World Health Organization. (2021). *Global strategy on digital health 2020-2025*. Retrieved from https://www.who.int/docs/default-source/documents/gs4dhdaa2a9f 352b0 445bafbc79ca799dce4d.pdf

178. Xu, Q., Leong, J., Qi Yi Chua, Yu Chung Tse, Pierce, Pack, D., & Wang, C.-H. (2013). Combined modality doxorubicin-based chemotherapy and chitosan-mediated p53 gene therapy using double-walled microspheres for treatment of human hepatocellular carcinoma. *Biomaterials*, *34*(21), 5149–5162. https://doi.org/10.1016/j.biomaterials.2013.03.044

179. Xu, Y., Wang, Q., An, Z., Wang, F., Zhang, L., Wu, Y., … Roepman, R. (2021). Artificial Intelligence: A Powerful Paradigm for Scientific Research. *The Innovation*, *2*(4), 100179. Sciencedirect. Retrieved from https://www.sciencedirect.com/science/article/pii/S2666675821001041

180. Yang, Z., Ren, J., Zhang, Z., Sun, Y., Zhang, C., Wang, M., & Wang Li-ya. (2023). A New Three-Way Incremental Naive Bayes Classifier. *Electronics*, *12*(7), 1730–1730. https://doi.org/10.3390/electronics12071730

181. Yoon, H. J., Jeong, Y. J., Kang, H., Jeong, J. E., & Kang, D.-Y. (2019). Medical Image Analysis Using Artificial Intelligence. *Korean Society of Medical Physics*, *30*(2), 49–58. https://doi.org/10.14316/pmp.2019.30.2.49

List of Abbreviations

ADHD	Attention Deficit Hyperactivity Disorder
ABDM	Ayushman Bharat Digital Mission
ABHA	Ayushman Bharat Health Account
ADMET	Absorption, Distribution, Metabolism, Excretion, and Toxicity
AI	Artificial Intelligence
AIM	Artificial Intelligence in Medicine
ALCOA+	Attributable, Legible, Contemporaneous, Original, Accurate, and Complete
AML	Acute Myeloid Leukaemia
ANNs	Artificial Neural Networks
APIs	Application Programming Interfaces
Apps	Applications
AUC-ROC	Area Under the Receiver Operating Characteristic Curve
BBB	Bioinformatics, Bioprocessing and Biomanufacturing
BML	Bayesian Machine learning
BT	Bluetooth technology
CAD	Computer-Aided Diagnosis
CADD	Computer-Aided Drug Design
CAI	Connectionist Artificial Intelligence
CAPE	Community-Acquired Pneumonia and COVID-19 Artificial Intelligence Predictive Engine
CBT	Cognitive Behavioral Therapy
CD	Clinical Data
CDD	Computational Drug Design
CDS	Clinical Decision Support
CE	Conformité Européenne
CGH	Changi General Hospital
CGM	Continuous glucose monitor
CMap	Connectivity Map
CNNs	Convolution Neural Networks
COVID-19	Corona Virus Disease 2019

CPS	Cyber-Physical System
CRVS	Civil Registration and Vital Statistics
CT	Computed Tomography
CVDs	Cardiovascular Diseases
DCTs	Decentralized Clinical Trials
DGIdb	Drug-Gene Interaction Database
DHI	Digital Health Intervention
DHIs	Digital Health Initiatives
DHTs	Digital Health Technologies
DILIrank	Drug-Induced Liver Injury Rank
DL	Deep Learning
DME	Diabetic Macular Edema
DNNs	Deep Neural Networks
DP	Data Pruning
DR	Diabetic Retinopathy
DT	Digital Technologies
DTx	Digital Therapeutics
EAI	Evolutionary Artificial Intelligence
EC	European Commission
EHR	Electronic Health Records
ELMIS	Electronic Logistics Management Information System
EMR	Electronic Medical Records
GAI	General Artificial Intelligence
GDP	Good Distribution Practices
GDPR	General Data Protection Rule
GENE-TOX	Genetic Toxicology Data Bank
GEO	Gene Expression Omnibus
GHODR	Global Health Observatory Data Repository
GIS	Geographic Information Systems
GMP	Good Manufacturing Practices
GoI	Government of India
GPS	Global Positioning System
GPUs	Graphics Processing Units
HCPs	Healthcare Providers
HFR	Health Facility Registry
HIE	Health Information Exchange
HIPAA	Health Insurance Portability and Accountability Act

HIS	Hospital Information Systems
HMSP	Digital Health Interventions Health Management and Support Personnel
HPR	Healthcare Professionals Registry
HTS	High-Throughput Screening
ICD	Implanted Cardioverter Defibrillator
ICU	Intensive Care Unit
IoMT	Internet of Medical Things
iOS	iPhone Operating System
IR	Industrial Revolution
IRNF	Irregular Rhythm Notification Feature
ISPE	International Society for Pharmaceutical Engineering
LAI	Limited Memory Artificial Intelligence
LBVS	Ligand-based virtual screening
LINCS	Library of Integrated Network-based Cellular Signatures
MCPS	Medical Cyber-Physical Systems
MDR	Manage Detection And Response
MDs	Medical Devices
mHealth	Mobile Health
MIA	Medical Image Analysis
MIT	Massachusetts Institute of Technology
ML	Machine Learning
MRI	Magnetic Resonance Imaging
MTM	Medication Therapy Management
NAI	Narrow Artificial Intelligence
NB	Naive Bayesian
NIH	National Institutes of Health
NLP	Natural Language Processing
NN	Neural networks
OHDSI	Observational Health Data Sciences and Informatics
PCA	Principal Component Analysis
PDB	Protein Data Bank
PET	Positron Emission Tomography
PHIs	Public Health Institutions
PM	Principia Mathematica
QbD	Quality by Design
QoL	Quality of Life

R&D	Research and Development
RAI	Reactive Artificial Intelligence
RAISE	Robotics, Automation, and Interfaces Scheduling Engine
RF	Random Forest
RL	Reinforcement Learning
RoMi-H	Robotics Middleware for Healthcare
ROS	Robot Operating System
RPM	Remote Patient Monitoring
RWD	Real-World Data
RWE	Real-world evidence
SAAI	Self-Aware Artificial Intelligence
SAI	Super Artificial Intelligence
SaMD	Software as Medical Devices
SAR	Structure-Activity Relationships
SBVS	Structure-Based Virtual Screening
SD	Sensor Data
SDSs	Safety Data Sheets
SET	Predictive Safety, Efficacy and Toxicity
SIDER	Side Effect Resource
SL	Supervised Learning
SMPD	Small Molecule Pathway Database
SMS	Short Message Service
SSL	Semi-supervised Learning
SVMs	Support Vector Machines
SWOT	Strengths, Weaknesses, Opportunities, Threats
SyAI	Symbolic Artificial Intelligence
TCGA	The Cancer Genome Atlas
TENS	Transcutaneous Electrical Nerve Stimulation
TMAI	Theory-of-Mind Artificial Intelligence
TTD	Therapeutic Target Database
UL	Unsupervised Learning
US	United States
VS	Virtual Screening
WHT	Wearable Health Technology

www.ingramcontent.com/pod-product-compliance
Lightning Source LLC
Chambersburg PA
CBHW071225230926
51849CB00001B/26
* 9 7 8 9 3 4 8 7 3 4 4 3 3 *